*TWAYNE'S WORLD AUTHORS SERIES*

*A Survey of the World's Literature*

Sylvia E. Bowman, Indiana University
GENERAL EDITOR

# RUSSIA

Nicholas P. Vaslef, U.S. Air Force Academy
EDITOR

## Konstantin Batyushkov

*(TWAS 287)*

*Novosti Press Agency, Publishing House, Moscow, USSR*

# KONSTANTIN BATYUSHKOV

# Konstantin Batyushkov

### By ILYA Z. SERMAN

*Institute of Russian Literature, Academy of Sciences of the USSR (Pushkin House)*

Twayne Publishers, Inc.   ::   New York

# *Preface*

Konstantin Nikolaevich Batyushkov is, it must be assumed, known only to a very limited circle of connoisseurs and lovers of Russian poetry. Yet, his creative, artistic innovations were organically assimilated into the *oeuvre* of Alexander Pushkin. Moreover, Batyushkov, together with Vasily Zhukovsky, is firmly established as one of the most important predecessors and teachers of the young Pushkin. This attitude to Batyushkov was most succintly expressed by Vissarion Belinsky, who wrote of Batyushkov in 1843 that he had bequeathed to the Russian poetry of his time "the beauty of ideal form."[1] In this definition of Batyushkov's historical role there is much truth, although the significance of his poetic work was not confined to the attainment of "ideal form." The fact remains that it was Batyushkov and not Pushkin who created classic Russian verse, that poetical form which still today, a century and a half after its first appearance, remains and will most probably long continue to be the basis of Russian prosody. Of course, before Batyushkov, Russian poetry had already achieved a high degree of perfection in the odes of Mikhail Lomonosov and the fables of Alexander Sumarokov. Batyushkov was the younger contemporary of a poet of genius—Gavriil Derzhavin; he learned much from Ivan Dmitriev and Nikolay Karamzin. Yet, between Batyushkov, or rather between Batyushkov's mature poetry and the poetry of the majority of his predecessors, there is a noticeable difference.

Eighteenth-century poetry, even at its best, never found a single style fitted to express the whole gamut of poetic themes. There was a very distinct difference between the "high" genres (the ode, the tragedy, the epic poem) and the "low" genres (the fable, the comedy, the satire). The concept of an individual poetic style did not yet exist either in theory or in practice.

Batyushkov can justly claim this distinction in Russian literature. He and no other confirmed the poet's right to his own, unrepeatable, individual, peculiar poetic style, which makes itself felt equally in his every poem, his every line. The unity of style in Batyushkov's poetry is the outward verbal expression of the unity of psychological tone and, in the last analysis, of the unity of the poet's personality, which makes itself felt as much throughout his whole work as in any one separate poem.

As a result, the ideal beauty of form in Batyushkov's poetry was subjected to a new content; it expressed a new feeling for the world born of that historical situation to which the poet owed his first conscious impressions.

The epoch in which Batyushkov was destined to live and write was one of the most significant turning points in the history of Europe and Russia. Batyushkov was born two years before the French Revolution of 1789. As a young man he fought in Russia's wars against Napoleon, and he was 27 years old in 1814 when he witnessed the surrender of Paris to the allied forces.

The complexity and contradictory nature of his epoch, the spectacle of political and social change constantly unfolding predetermined the very character of his poetic quest, his conviction as to the necessity of a radical change in Russian poetry and his intense work to create new means of expression for the thoughts and feelings of his contemporaries. In this, above all, lies the true significance of Batyushkov in the history of Russian poetry. And this is why, in this book, the author endeavors, on the one hand, to show how Batyushkov built up and elaborated his own poetic style, his sources, the difficulties he had to overcome, by what devious routes he sometimes had to travel and, on the other, to determine what part of his poetic heritage still lives on today, what has remained and will always remain alive for poetry lovers.

In the first chapter of this book an attempt is made to describe the literary and social conditions under which Batyushkov embarked on his poetic work when he was still a disciple of Karamzin and Dmitriev. The second chapter traces Batyushkov's orientation in the literary and social movements and the political struggle of the first two decades of the nineteenth century. The third and fourth chapters follow the process by which Batyushkov came to create his own poetic style. Chapter 5 is devoted to the most important genre in his poetry, the elegy, in which Batyushkov's poetic talent and artistic originality found their most vivid expression. Chapter 6 contains an analysis of the only collection of works edited by the poet himself: *Essays in Verse and Prose* (*Opyty v stikhakh i proze*, 1817). It goes on to examine the search for new approaches begun after the publication of *Essays*, but soon interrupted by psychological illness. In the "Conclusion," a brief sketch is given of Batyushkov's place in Russian poetry during the first quarter of the nineteenth century, his attitude to the Romantic movement and his influence on the further development of Russian poetry.

ILYA Z. SERMAN

*Leningrad*

# Contents

# Chronology

KONSTANTIN BATYUSHKOV

(*Ten' druga*) and *On the Ruins of a Castle in Sweden* (*Na razvali-nakh zamka v Shvetsii*).

1815    Returns from leave to Kamenets-Podolsk where unit is stationed. Writes great deal in prose: composes an elegaic cycle: *My genius* (*Moy geniy*), *Separation* (*Razluka*), *Tavrida, Hope* (*Nadezhda*), *To a Friend* (*K drugu*), *Awakening* (*Probuzhdenie*); translates Charles-Hubert Millevoye's *La chute des feuilles* as *The Last Spring* (*Poslednaya vesna*).

1816    Arrives in Moscow. Retires from army. Accepted as member of Moscow Society of Lovers of Literature (*Moskovskoe obshchestvo Lyubitiley slovesnosti*). Writes *A Discourse on the Influence of Light Verse on Language* (*Rech'o vliyanii legkoy poezii na yazyk*), later printed in his *Works* (*Trudy*). Sells publication rights of prose and verse to Gnedich, prepares first volume for print. Writes *An Evening with Kantemir* (*Vecher u Kantemira*), poem *The Song of Harold the Bold* (*Pesn' Garol'da Smelogo*), and translation from Millevoye's *Combat d'Homère et d'Hésiode*. Takes up residence in Khantonova.

1817    Prepares second (verse) volume of his *Essays*. Visits St. Petersburg in summer and attends meetings of Arzamas literary circle. Writes *The Crossing of the Rhine* (*Perekhod cherez Reyn*), *The Dying Tasso* (*Umirayushchiy Tass*), *The Bower of the Muses* (*Besedka muz*), *From a Greek Anthology* (*Iz grecheskoy antologii*). Second (verse) volume of *Essays* published and favorably received by critics.

1818    Arranges to enter the Diplomatic Service. Leaves for Naples in November.

1819–    Diplomatic Service in Naples and Rome. Friendship with Russian
1820    artists. Health begins to fail.

1821–    Takes sick leave. Returns to St. Petersburg. Goes to Crimea for treat-
1822    ment.

1823    Persecution mania. Burns his books. Makes three attempts to commit suicide.

1824–    Undergoes course of treatment at Sonnenstein psychiatric hospital
1827    in Saxony.

1828–    Lives with relatives in Moscow.
1832

1833–    Lives with relatives in town of Vologda—an incurably sick man.
1855

1855    Dies of typhus on July 19th.

### CHAPTER 1

# The Poet's Youth

## I  *First Experiences*

ON May 18, 1787 a long-awaited son was born to Nikolay Lvovich and Alexandra Grigorevna Batyushkov in the town of Vologda. Konstantin, as he was named, was the youngest of a family of four daughters. The eldest sister, Alexandra Nikolaevna, was soon to take the place of the mother in the family, for Alexandra Grigorevna fell victim to a serious mental illness and was taken to Petersburg where, in 1795, she died. It was evidently from his mother that Konstantin Batyushkov inherited a predisposition to nervous ailments to which he was subject throughout his life. This psychic instability was finally to prove the poet's undoing when, at the age of thirty-five, he succumbed to insanity.

Konstantin Batyushkov spent his childhood on the family estate in the village of Danilovskoe, where the manor house, situated on top of a steep bank overlooking a river, stands to this day. The Batyushkov family was of the old nobility, and its members, although never distinguished by wealth or influence, had filled various state offices since the sixteenth century. The life of the poet's father was clouded by his involvement in court proceedings against an uncle, who was exiled to Siberia in 1770 for attempting to dethrone the Empress Catherine II. Nikolay Lvovich was involved only to the extent of being a witness, but was nevertheless dismissed from the army and exiled to his estate. In Danilovskoe, he lived in almost unbroken seclusion and occupied himself diligently, though without marked success, with managing his estate. An educated man for his time, he built up a well-stocked library, consisting mainly of the works of French eighteenth century writers and philosophers. Wishing to give his son a good education, Nikolay Lvovich took Konstantin to Petersburg and left him at a private boarding school of good repute, run by a Monsieur Jacquinot, a native of Alsace. The program of studies was designed to give the education and polish required of young men of good families destined to take their places in aristocratic society. The annual cost per student at the Pensionnat Jacquinot was 700 rubles—a considerable sum of money in those days, which automatically made the school exclusive, limiting its pupils to the sons of the richer nobility. The pupils studied divinity, Russian, French, German, geography, history, statistics (economic geography), arithmetic, chemistry, botany, calligraphy, drawing, and dancing.

For four years Batyushkov studied at Jacquinot's, and then for another year at the Pensionnat Tripoli where, in addition to the subjects already mentioned, he received instruction in the Italian language. In his later life, Batyushkov never reminisced either about his childhood or his school years, and his school years did not seem to be particularly happy ones. Still, the most important aspect of his education, as for every inquiring-minded adolescent, was reading. In the Pensionnat Jacquinot, most subjects were taught in French, and it is little wonder that French literature, together with Russian and German, and later Italian constituted his reading.

Batyushkov began writing poetry while at the boarding school. Two lines of one early attempt, written when he was fifteen years old, Batyushkov later quoted in a letter to Gnedich.

> *Dlya nas vsyo khorosho vdali,*
> *Vblizi—vsyo skuchno i postylo!*
>
> For us all things afar are fair,[1]
> The near at hand—flat and distasteful!

After he left the pensionnat, Batyushkov took up the study of Latin and began to read the Roman poets.

After completing his education in 1802, Batyushkov settled in St. Petersburg in the house of his uncle, Mikhail Nikitich Muraryov, who obtained a position for him at the newly-created Ministry of Public Education. Work as a civil servant held no charm for Batyushkov, but thanks to the patronage of his uncle in whose office he held a sinecure as clerk, young Konstantin was able to abandon himself to all the pleasures of social life in the capital and to indulge his taste for poetry, writing verses at work instead of copying official papers.

Batyushkov's appointment to the Ministry of Public Education brought him into contact with a wide circle of literary figures. Among those who served with him were several young, but already quite well known writers and poets. One of these, Ivan Petrovich Pnin (1773–1805), was the author of a treatise on *The Experience of Enlightenment With Regard to Russia* (*Opyt o prosveshchenii otnositel'no Rossii,* 1804) and was also the founder of the *St. Petersburg Journal* (*Sanktpeterburgsky zhurnal*) (1798). A poet and publicist convinced of the benefits of Enlightenment, Pnin was a close associate of the revolutionary writer Alexander Nikolaevich Radishchev. One of the young men who worked with Batyushkov was Radishchev's son, Nikolay Alexandrovich (1774–1829), an educated young man with some talent for letters, with whom Batyushkov kept up friendly relations for many years. Nikolay Ivanovich Gnedich (1784–1833), a novelist and poet, who became Batyushkov's closest friend, was also one of his fellow employees at the Ministry.

The five years from 1802–1807 were a period of growing maturity and serious self-improvement for Batyushkov, the results of which became evident only in the following decade. Batyushkov continued to write poetry and, in 1805, his colleagues at work coaxed him into joining "The Free Society of Literature, Sciences and Arts" (*Vol'noe Obshchestvo slovesnosti, nauk i khudozhestv*). From that year, his verses began to appear in print, mostly in the publications of the Society. When Pnin died of tuberculosis, Batyushkov, Radishchev and other members of the "Free Society" wrote verses on his death.

As a youth, Batyushkov was torn between his poetic aspirations and the necessity of maintaining his sinecure by having to spend time on the intolerably wearisome task of copying boring official papers. "I hate the civil service,"[2] he confided to one of his friends. Later, approving of Gnedich's renunciation of a career in the civil service, Batyushkov wrote to him:

Had you continued to serve amid the dust and ashes, copying in full, copying excerpts, filling whole quires of paper with line upon line of copy, bowing first to the left, then to the right, progressing after the fashion of toads and grassnakes, you would by now have been Someone, but you did not choose to lose your freedom and gave penury and Homer the preference over money.[3]

Poetry and creative work monopolized his thoughts and his time.

His early verses are evidence of his attempts at various styles, imitating the manners of totally dissimilar Russian and French poets: Derzhavin, Dmitriev, Radishchev, Gresset, and Parny. The subjects of his verses differ widely: they include satirical pictures of the aristocratic society, such as *A Letter to Chloe* (*Poslanie k Khloe*) *A Translation of Boileau's Fourth Satire* (*Perevod 4-oy satiry Bualo*), *To Filice* (*K Filise*), all written between 1804 and 1805, and philosophic meditations in the spirit of Derzhavin such as *God* (*Bog*) in 1805.

The main theme at this time, however, was poetry itself. Batyushkov wanted to understand and define the essence of poetry—its place in the life of man and society, its function and its goal. In poetry he saw the only means of escape from the abhorrent existence he was leading under the yoke of his bureaucratic duties. Only poetry was capable of transporting man to a world created by his own imagination, to that world of dreams where alone he might realize his conception of the fullness of life and the harmonious and beautiful human being. This is why dreaming—as the most significant definition of the essence of poetry—is the most constant motif of Batyushkov's verses between 1802 and 1807.

In poets of all nations Batyushkov perceives only dreamers, such as Ossian, poet of the Northern scene whom he mentions in the very first of his known verses *Dream* (*Mechta*) 1802–1803. The bards of Europe's Southern shores, the poets of Greece and Rome, are dreamers, too, in Batyushkov's eyes. Even such an optimistic, earthy, and joyously sensual poet as Evariste Parny is transformed by Batyushkov's translations into a dreamer. In his translation of Parny's elegy *Que le bonheur arrive lentement,*[4] after the first two lines Batyushkov inserts two of his own, having nothing whatever in common with the original:

> *Kak schast'e medlenno prikhodit,*
> *Kak skoro proch'ot nas letit!*
> *Blazhen, za nim kto ne bezhit,*
> No sam v sebo ego nakhodit![5]

> How swiftly happines is over,
> How long we wait her tardy grace!
> Most happy, who refuse the chase,
> *And in themselves true joy discover!*

Further he inserts several mentions of dreaming and of happiness in dreams, and rearranges Parny to suit his own conception of the poet dreamer.

This basic mood of Batyushkov's early poetry was not original. The inexperienced poet was enthusiastically developing a theme which occupied a significant place in the poetry and prose of Karamzin and in the verses of Dmitriev. Nikolay M. Karamzin (1766–1826) had been the first Russian theoretician and practitioner of the concept of poetry as a sphere of the imagination. He saw in poetry a form of expression for the thoughts and feelings of man which could compensate for the failings and imperfections of reality by substituting the ideals of a beautiful human being and a harmonious existence. This concept of the essence of poetry was particularly characteristic of the Sentimentalist Karamzin in the mid-1790's, although later, he somewhat changed his views.

The other acknowledged master of Russian Sentimentalism, Ivan I. Dmitriev (1760–1837), was also at the end of his poetic career. Derzhavin, still alive, was writing his *Anacreontic Songs* (*Anakreonticheskie pesni*) which were published as a separate collection in 1804. The crystallization of literary trends which took place during the early years of the century created a favorable atmosphere for the appearance of Admiral Alexander Semyonovich Shishkov's book *Discussion of the Old and New Style of the Russian Language* (*Rassuzhdenie o novom i starom sloge,* 1803), directed against Karamzin's literary reform. Shishkov maintained that Karamzin's prose style was founded on incorrect principles in investing Russian words with new meanings corresponding to French post-Revolutionary terminology. Shishkov supported his stylistic criticisms with political arguments and depicted Karamzin—a conservative and a staunch supporter of autocracy—as a revolutionary and a disruptive force.

In the literary polemics for and against Karamzin, which arose after the appearance of Shiskov's book, Batyushkov took the side of Karamzin. In his *Letter to my Verses* (*Poslanie k stikham moim,* 1804–1805), Batyushkov ridiculed Shishkov and poets of similar persuasion. Shiskhov's appeal to renounce the new ideas and to return to the traditions and imagery of ancient Russian literature and its Church Slavonic language was quite unacceptable and provoked the most vigorous opposition. Batyushkov accepted neither the imitators of Karamzin nor of Derzhavin. He ridiculed both the authors of laudatory odes and the lacrimose emulators of Karamzin. Much more difficult, however, was the establishment of a platform of his own. He realized that as a poet he had done nothing more than consolidate the gains of his predecessors and, because of this, his letters and verses of that period often voice doubts as to his vocation and the measure of his poetic talent.

## II   *Literary Influences*

Batyushkov's talent developed differently from what might have been expected on the basis of his early work. The poet's introduction to the literary and artistic circle which met at the home of Alexey Olenin had a significant influence on his literary tastes. Alexey Nikolaevich Olenin (1763–1843) was a connoisseur of art history and archaeology, an artist in his own right, Director of the Public Library from 1811 and President of the Academy of Arts from 1817. His home was a gathering place for writers connected with the theater and for artists. Gnedich was an old friend of the family and presumably he introduced Batyushkov to this circle. Other regular visitors to the Olenins were the fabulist, Ivan Andreevich Krylov, the playwright, Vladislav Alexandrovich Ozerov, and Alexander Alexandrovich Shakhovskoy. The talk at Olenin's home helped form and develop Batyushkov's literary and artistic opinions. He found he had much in common with Olenin's own views on art. Like Olenin, he accepted J. J. Winckelmann as his aesthetic mentor in his approach to antique art and, like Gnedich, he believed that a deep understanding of the spirit of antique art was essential to the artist. Olenin and Gnedich believed that it was possible to establish a direct connection between the laws and secrets of Greek and contemporary Russian art and poetry. In their opinion, Russian artistic culture might be recreated as a distinctly national and truly Russian culture by injecting certain elements of Greek culture. Not imitation, but assimilation; creative reapplication of basic principles was the way which would lead to a synthesis of the Greek heritage with Russian themes, characters, and subjects.

In spite of the paradox inherent in this idea, it was, in many ways, justified by results. Russian sculpture, architecture, and, to some extent, Russian poetry between 1810 and 1820 by following this very road, was to achieve a great deal and to create a particular epoch in the history of Russian art, an epoch of masterpieces unsurpassed in many respects.[6] Later, from the 1840's on, this synthesis of antique form and Russian—or so-called Russian—content degenerated into lifeless academism, into monotonous, uninspired imitativeness. In 1810, however, this trend in Russian art was alive and fruitful. Neither Olenin nor Gnedich considered it possible that Russian art should imitate the Ancients. On the contrary, Gnedich subjected all eighteenth century literature to severe criticism for its tendency to imitate either German ("they strummed out their magnificent odes on Gothic lyres") or French models ("they founded . . . their epics on the insufficient edifice of the French narrative poem").[7] According to Gnedich, the art of the Ancient World in general, and Greek poetry in particular, required a correct historical interpretation in the spirit of Johann Joachim Winckelmann and Johann Gottfried von Herder as the organic expression of the true nature of man in his time, an epoch of especially harmonious relations between man and society, and between art and reality. Thus, several years later, Gnedich formulated his conception of what the relationship between Russian art and Classical poetry should be.

"There can be no doubt," he wrote "that to set up Ancient literature to be in every way a model for our own would be the same thing as to seek to lend our world the image of the Ancient World. It is inevitable that there should be a difference between Ancient and Modern times, and the difference between the poetries of these times is natural. However, Ancient and Modern literature alike are subject to one and the same law of taste: and the Modern, acknowledging her rival to be most excellent, should elect her as a model of unity, truth, power, and simplicity, especially in poetry: for in poetry no one can excel the Greeks."[8]

Thus, Gnedich suggested not so much that Russian poets should imitate the Greeks, but that they should be faithful to "the truth" and seek to achieve "power and simplicity," that is, to create a heroic civil poetry based on national and historic Russian traditions.

Arguing against the imitative Sentimentalism of Karamzin's followers, Gnedich called for naturalness, again citing Greek poetry: "Only the Greeks knew how to be at once natural and original. All other peoples tried to improve or change nature herself after their own fashion—to substitute sentimentality for sentiment, refinement for simplicity."[9] Gnedich's translations, in particular his work on the Russian translation of the *Iliad,* was a way by which he hoped to come to a poetic style suitable for the creation of a heroic national epic poetry.[10]

At the time Batyushkov entered Olenin's circle, his great interest was the theater. Gnedich, too, was working for the theater, translating the tragedies of Voltaire and Jean-François Ducis, but his main interest at this time was learning and rehearsing parts with the great Russian actress Ekaterina Semyonova, whose genius brought a period of flowering to tragic drama in Russia between 1810 and 1820. In Olenin's circle the dramatic talent of Vladislav Ozerov, the renovator of Russian tragedy, matured and thrived. At the time Batyushkov joined the circle, the interests of its members were concentrated on Ozerov's tragedies *Oedipus in Athens* (*Edip V Afinakh,* 1804) and *Fingal* (1805). The treatment of political problems in eighteenth century tragedies did not count on the recognition of ideas behind the actual words or on the unraveling of hints, but on an intense reaction to the emotional and psychological content of the text. The tears and compassion of the audience were for the tragic heroes as individuals, rather than for the fate of the country or the nation.

Ozerov's tragedies were extremely well-written works. They were distinguished from the tragedies of Sumarokov and Knyazhnin by the predominance of the lyrical over the dramatic element, and the antique mythological or borrowed literary subjects served as a form through which to express modern sentiments.

The writing of Ozerov's tragedies coincided with the beginning of a new era during which Russia was to be drawn into a European war—the struggle of the peoples of Europe against Napoleon. Although little changed in form, Russian tragedy became a center of topical allusion, a mirror of the political passions and emotions of the day.

The astounding success of Ozerov's *Oedipus in Athens* is explained by the fact that an apparently far from modern subject was understood as a direct reaction to the political situation in Russia. The audiences understood the monologues of Theseus as discourses on the attitude of Alexander I preparing to enter the war against Napoleon on the side of England and Austria. More than this, in justifying Oedipus' parricide by depicting him as an "involuntary" transgressor, Ozerov implied that the Russian nation forgives Alexander I for his parricide, thus expressing society's confidence in the new monarch. This is why the fate of the involuntary transgressor, Oedipus, so deeply touched the Russian people in 1804–1805. The audience watching the tragedy on the stage was reexperiencing the recent political tragedy—the assassination of Paul I—still fresh in every one's mind, and for which some still blamed Alexander I. Only this direct application of the antique myth to contemporary life can explain the tears and enthusiasm of the spectators of *Oedipus in Athens.*

The phenomenal success of Ozerov's tragedies on stage made him many enemies, among them Derzhavin, who at that time had taken sides with Shishkov. The triumphant reception of Ozerov's new tragedy coincided with Batyushkov's departure from St. Petersburg, and he sent his friends the fable of *The Shepherd and the Nightingale* (*Pastukh i solovey*) in which he enjoined the playwright to go on with his "singing" and not to listen to "the frogs" from "the marshes close by," who in the fable are doing their best to drown the voice of the "nightingale."

By 1807, these literary and theatrical storms which Batyushkov had followed so attentively, began to be pushed into the back of his mind by the great historical events into which Russia was now drawn.


### III   *The Poet at War*

In 1805 Napoleon routed the forces of the Russo-Austrian coalition at Austerlitz. Russia, in alliance now with Prussia, was preparing for a new war. The enemy was known to be very strong and the government had to resort to emergency measures. On November 30, 1806 it was decided to create a Volunteer Corps or Militia as a reserve for the Army. Infected by the general spirit of patriotism, Batyushkov, without waiting for his father's permission, took a commission as officer in a battalion of the St. Petersburg Militia and in February 1807, set out for the front in the best of spirits. His letters to Gnedich from the campaign are full of jokes, questions about the latest literary news from St. Petersburg, and the desire to come to grips with the French at the first possible opportunity. This desire was soon satisfied. At the victorious battle of Heilsberg on May 29, 1807, he was seriously wounded in the leg. More dead than alive, Batyushkov was transported by cart to Riga, where he was taken into the home of a wealthy citizen, and permitted to remain there until his wound was healed. On his recovery he returned home to Danilovskoe where he was confronted by his father's remarriage, greatly resented by the grown-up children of his first wife since it adversely affected their material welfare.

Meanwhile the Treaty of Tilsit had ended the war against Napoleon. Batyushkov, however, decided not to leave military service and obtained a transfer to the Guards Regiment of Jaegers (Riflemen). He spent the winter of 1807–1808 in St. Petersburg, suffering from rather poor health, but still being able to continue as a member of Olenin's circle. In May, 1808, he was sent to Finland where war had broken out against the Swedes. Military activities went on until May, 1809. Of the important operations during this war, Batyushkov was involved only in crossing the ice over the Gulf of Bothnia, leading to the occupation of the Aland Islands. When activities ceased, Batyushkov left for the village of Khantonovo where his sisters were now living and, at the end of the year, retired from the service, believing that he had been unfairly passed over for promotion.

The summer and autumn of 1809 which Batyushkov spent in retirement in the country were, in spite of the complaints of boredom and depression in his letters to his friends, extremely fruitful for his poetical work. Here Batyushkov achieved his own poetical self-determination, his emancipation from the influences of others, and the establishment of his own position in literature. And at this time Batyushkov came out with his boldest statement on contemporary literature in the satirical poem *A Vision on the Shores of the Lethe* (*Videnie na beregakh Lete*).

Between his period of dreams, with repetitions of the poetic themes common to all Russian Sentimentalism, and *A Vision on the Shores of the Lethe*, in which the poet settled accounts not only with the surviving followers of Sentimentalism, but also with his own past, was the experience of two wars—an important period in Batyushkov's intellectual development.

War, with all its painful and distressing experiences, had proved a serious formative influence on the young poet. When he first entered military service in 1806, Batyushkov had been only nineteen years old. For a youth of such naturally sensitive and impressionable temperament, the campaigns, battles, wounds, the deaths of his comrades, could not but have the most powerful effect on his growth toward spiritual maturity. Even in the restrained, rather dry and ironic style of Batyushkov's letters to his regular correspondent of those years, Nikolay Gnedich, it can be felt how profoundly and seriously the war had moved the young poet to think about the eternal problems of human existence and, most of all, about death. He wrote to Gnedich:

By the way, do you remember that Guards Officer you and I saw in the restaurant? Such a fine young fellow. He was killed. Such is our lot. We have also lost two of the best officers from our own battalion. *Nothing makes one think so much as frequent visits from Madame Death.* Let your brother scribblers crown her with roses; indeed, she is far from amusing for those who have to endure her company.[11]

One consequence of these innermost thoughts and reexamination of his previous attitude to poetry was the reworking of earlier poems and the writing of *A Vision on the Shores of the Lethe* (1809), establishing Batyushkov's reputation among his contemporaries as a mature and original poet.

By the irony of its manner and style, this poem was a new phenomenon not only in the work of Batyushkov, but in Russian poetry. The confidence and freedom with which the young poet parodies and ridicules the style of some of his contemporaries would seem amazingly unexpected were it not for those letters of Batyushkov to Gnedich from which we can trace the elaboration of the poetic manner so brilliantly exploited in *A Vision on the Shores of the Lethe*.

These letters, while they contain a good deal of factual information, are of a rather particular character. They are the epistles of a poet to a poet, literary through and through. Batyushkov is as interested in the "how" as in the "what" of communication. If Batyushkov's letters to Gnedich are compared with those written over the same period to his sister Alexandra Nikolaevna, the basic difference between them immediately strikes the reader.

In June 1807, Batyushkov wrote to both Gnedich and to his sisters telling them of the same event—his serious wound at the battle of Heilsberg, his agonizing journey on the cart, and his blissful stay in Riga. The facts recounted are the same, but the way in which those facts are set forth—or, more precisely, the writer's

attitude to those facts—change according to his correspondent.
The letters to his sisters are half in Russian and half in French. The
letters to Gnedich are in Russian only. To his sisters he writes:
"Dear sisters, By the Grace of God I am feeling well, although
wounded by a ball in the hip which passed through the body
without touching the bone."[12] The tone of the letter to Gnedich
is quite different: "Good friend! I am alive. How—God knows.
I was seriously wounded in the leg by a ball which passed in through
the upper thigh and out by the bottom. The wound is two quarters
deep, but not dangerous because the bone, they say, was untouch-
ed, though how?—again, I do not know."[13] God, who is mentioned
in passing in the letters to Gnedich, occupies a more fitting place
in the letters to Batyushkov's sister: "I was in considerable pain
on the road from Prussia, but now, thanks to the Almighty, Who
helped to save and preserve my life, I am in the most hospitable
house that ever existed. . . . And I bless the Eternal one Who has
preserved my life for your sakes, my dear friends."[14]

The letter to the sisters goes on in the same tone, whereas the one
to Gnedich runs on into jokes and witticisms: "May Aesculapians
declare that I shall go lame for a whole year. And though I say so
myself, I am extremely comical on my crutches."[15]

The friendly, joking, and ironic tone of this letter, evident here
only occasionally because of the extraordinary circumstances
under which it was written, constitutes the basic mood of Batyushkov's other letters. Their other peculiarity is that they were written
in a mixture of prose and verse.

At the beginning of the campaign Batyushkov wrote Gnedich,
deliberately stylizing his letters: "I expect even your drunken
Achilles never downed as much wine and vodka as I on this campaign; write to me, in verse if you like; the Muses deserted me as
from the Red Tavern. Now in Riga, at least, let me hear an echo
of your minstrelsy."[16] From this letter it is quite obvious that
here we have one poet addressing another poet. The joking tone
of the letter is established by the unexpected juxtaposition of
officers and drinking bouts on campaign with "your" Achilles, who
was, of course, the constant object of Gnedich's attention in his
poetic labors as translator of Homer's *Iliad*. The facetious tone
of the reference to Achilles prepares the way for the next joke

about the Muses who have deserted Batyushkov as from the Red Tavern, a famous inn on the outskirts of St. Petersburg.

The last prose appeal to friend and fellow-poet ("Now, in Riga, at least, let me hear an echo of your minstrelsy") is repeated, this time in verse:

> Must we but hark to the importunate drum?
> Let friendship again, soft-voiced slip by
> For but one hour unite with Parnassus
> Him who unthinkingly great Ares' cloak did don
> And with his Rosinante, famed in story,
> Jogged off, as best he could, in search of glory.[17]

Here, the joke and self-mockery are founded on a stylistic device employed throughout these friendly letters: lofty images established in literary usage are ironically reinterpreted: "Great Ares' cloak," donned all "unthinkingly," becomes a jesting periphrastic appellation for an officer's uniform. The familiarly conversational "nevznachay," meaning accidentally (translated here as "unthinkingly" in the sense of "carelessly," "without fixed intent"), lends everything of which Batyushkov is writing a touch of frivolity, flippancy, and buffoonery even though the subject of his verse is of considerable importance to him.

In the ensuing letters to Gnedich, Batyushkov gives still more space to poetry, to the literary news from St. Petersburg, and to his own verses:

Imagine my riding a chestnut horse over the open plains and happier than any king, for as I ride I recite Tasso or something else of that nature. It has been known to happen that, just as one raises one's voice in the words, Oh bravery divine, oh most heroic deeds!, one finds oneself landing with a thud on one's side, unhorsed. But what does it matter! Better be thrown by Bucephalus than, like Bobrov, take a tumble from Pegasus.[18]

Literary interests and news of the life and struggle on the literary front interest Batyushkov as much, if not more, than his military campaign. This is why the object of his derision is still Bobrov, the invariable butt of pro-Karamzin criticism and parodies, and why, in a letter to Olenin, Batyushkov begs his correspondent to remind his literary acquaintances—Ozerov, Kapnist, Krylov, Shakhovskoy:

> . . . that here's one poet who
> A prey to Fortune's changes
> Exiled from the fair founts of Helicon's high ranges,
> Must lay aside his lyre for rifle and for lance,
> Nor mend his quills but lend his sabre brighter glance,
> Must, with ferocious mien, take up his soldier's load
> And beetle-browed pursue a very boring road,
> A road where language sounds more like the cries of beasts,
> A dirty road which leads me, to my grief,
> Not to the temple of immortal glory
> But, maybe, to a dingy inn by the gates.[19]

The literary quality of Batyushkov's letters and the deliberate element of parody were more than a mere reflection of his interests. In his letter Batyushkov hints at the themes of his future verses and, most importantly, works out a new style, a peculiar type of free, unconstrained, outwardly "unliterary" exposition of the most serious poetic ideas closest to his heart. The literary quality of Batyushkov's letters led to the creation of new poetic genres in which the usual literary quality of existing genres was contrasted to the "unliterariness" of those he himself had elaborated. First and foremost among these was the friendly, epistolary poem. In *A Vision on the Shores of the Lethe*, the technique Batyushkov had earlier worked out in the odds and ends of verse in his letters—the comical juxtaposition of high, serious literary and mythological images with the kind of low, everyday matter hitherto reserved for comedy—was brilliantly exploited.


## IV  *Translating Torquato Tasso*

The process of inner transformation did not find expression in Batyushkov's works at first. From 1807 to 1808 he was still, to a considerable extent, under the influence of Olenin's circle and their ideas, one of which was the creation of a Russian national epos on the basis of studying and creatively reworking the epic poetry of other peoples. This is how Gnedich had begun work on the *Iliad*, and Batyushkov, under the influence of Olenin and Gnedich, undertook to translate the epic poem of the great Italian, Torquato Tasso, *Jerusalem Delivered*. This epic had enjoyed particular popularity at the turn of the eighteenth–nineteenth centuries among the French pre-Romantics and, later, the Romantics. The theoreticians of Romanticism, Madame de Staël and Sismondi, undertook to prove that Tasso, together with Shakespeare and Calderón, was one of the main forerunners of Romanticism.[20]

Tasso interested the Romantics equally by his work, whose variety was untamed by the leveling laws of French Classicism, as well as by his tragic fate, which they interpreted as an inevitable misfortune awaiting the poet at the hands of the hostile and uncomprehending Philistine. Jean-Jacques Rousseau had considered Tasso's biography, not only his poetry, to be poetical. This view was shared by Chateaubriand who imitated Tasso in his prose epic *The Martyrs* (1809). Earlier, in *The Genius of Christianity* (1802), he had written an apologia of Tasso as the poet of Christianity who, in his epic poem, had created the character of a beautiful warrior inspired by a high moral ideal.[21]

Batyushkov, in his *Epistle to N. I. Gnedich* (1805), repeated the general consensus of critical opinion at the beginning of the nineteenth century, which pronounced Tasso to be astonishingly diverse in the themes and images of his poetry:

> *Kak slavny Tass, volshebnoyu rukoy*
> *Yavlyaet divny khram prirody*[22]
> . . . . . . . . . . . . . . . . . . . . . . . . . . . .
> When glorious Tasso with magician's hand
> Reveals the wondrous temple of our World
> With Nature's various marvels all unfurled,
> Now black Hell meets my eyes,
> Now gardens of delight, Armida's paradise,
> But when the mighty deeds of heroes he is praising,
> A harsher voice in songs of battle raising,
> The weapons clash and boom, the wounded groan and screech. . . .
> For such is Poetry's speech!

At first Batyushkov appeared to take his work of translation seriously and translated the first part of *Jerusalem Delivered*. There is no copy of the translation extant. However, he soon relinquished his ambition of translating the entire grandiose epic and contented himself with publishing two episodes from it.

It is characteristic of Batyushkov that he continued to be interested in the work and the poetic manner of Tasso, as can be seen from his article *Ariosto and Tasso* (1815). At the same time, it is evident from this same article that the chief attraction of Tasso's poem for Batyushkov was not its epic subject nor the aspect of martial and religious heroism, but the actual poetic manner of Tasso: the variety and subtlety of Tasso's language and the total absence of all delimitations of style between genres. The regulating principle of Tasso's style was his will, that is, his personal attitude to one theme or another. In his article, Batyushkov wrote:

We cannot pause to particularize all the beauties of *Jerusalem Delivered:* they are legion! The enchanting episode of Erminia, the death of Clorinda, the gardens of Armida, and the single combat between Tancred and Argant. Who has read you without delight? You will remain unforgotten by all sensitive readers and all lovers of the beautiful! Yet in Tasso's poem there are beauties of another sort, and to these the poet and the critic alike should call attention. The description of folk customs and religious ceremonies is the most precious adjunct of epic poetry. Tasso excelled therein. With what art he depicted the manners of the knights, their generosity, their humility in victory, their unbelievable courage and piety![23]

When, after the epistle in verse *To Tasso*, Batyushkov printed an excerpt from the first canto of *Jerusalem Delivered*, he added the following note:

Perhaps amateurs of poetry will make allowances when they read this attempt to translate a few octaves from Tasso's immortal poem. If they fail to find high poetic thoughts, beauties of expression, melodious fluency of verse, it is the fault of the translator: the original is immortal.[24]

About a year later Batyushkov's feeling toward his translation changed in view of the general development and growing maturity of his literary tastes. In a letter to Gnedich he criticized the latter's translation of a certain canto from the *Iliad* and formulated his own general opinion on some aspects of the stylistic problems of epic poetry: "Rereading your translation, I become more and more persuaded that too much Slavonicizing is not necessary and will prove to be your undoing. . . . I also feel that certain particular Slavic words and turns of speech are quite out of place: you felt that yourself."

In criticizing his friend's translation, Batyushkov was in fact criticizing his own translation of Tasso, equally permeated by traditional examples of the high style. Apparently the difficulties which Batyushkov experienced while working on his *Jerusalem Delivered* had their origin in his desire to reproduce those features of Tasso's poetic style which were of most value to him as a translator. While sharing the general opinion of the French Romantics on Tasso's poetry, Batyushkov polemicized with them on one question which he felt to be extremely important: was the Italian language capable of expressing complex content, profound thoughts, and original ideas? Even Madame de Staël, one of the forerunners of the Romantic movement and an admirer of Tasso's poetry, was negative on these issues. Writing of Southern Romance literatures, she ventures the opinion:

The full sound of the Italian language does not predispose either the reader or the writer to think. Emotion puts even sensibility to rout in the face of the excessively magnificent harmonies. In the Italian language there is not sufficient precision for the expression of ideas, there is not sufficient vagueness for the expression of melancholy sentiments. It is a language of such extraordinary melodiousness that it seems to touch off musical chords, so that we do not pay attention to the actual meaning of the words: they affect us as would a musical instrument. On reading in Tasso such verses as:

> *Chiama gli abitator dell'ombre eterne*
> *Il rauco suon della tartarea tromba!*
> *Treman le spaziose atre caverne,*
> *E l'aer cieco a quel romor rimbomba . . .*
> From *Gerusalemme Liberata.* Canto IV, Stanza III.

No one could fail to be enchanted by them. At the same time, if one looks more closely at the sense of these words, it is impossible to find any lofty meaning in them.[25]

As if in answer to Madame de Staël, Batyushkov wrote in his article *Ariosto and Tasso*:

But the fortunate language of Italy, the richest heir to the ancient Latin, is accused of excessive effeminacy! This reproach is totally unjust and proves nothing but ignorance: specialists can point to many places in Tasso, in Ariosto . . . and in other writers of more or less renown, to many poems in which powerful and sublime thoughts are expressed in powerful sounds altogether suited to them, where language is the direct expression of a courageous soul filled with patriotism and love of freedom. Tasso's reputation does not rest exclusively on *Chiama gli abitator*: many other lines show the strength of the poet and the language.[26]

In his translation, Batyushkov evidently had not solved the problem of how to convey "the direct expression of the soul" of the poet through that traditional epic form in which he had confined the octaves of the Italian poet. Apparently, Batyushkov realized that the *grand genre* in poetry was not yet for him and that it was not right for him to undertake a task so foreign to his character and talent.

Abandoning his translation of Tasso's poem, Batyushkov composed a totally original long poem of his own, successfully finding a form for expressing his own, not borrowed, thoughts and feelings. As we know, this poem was his *A Vision on the Shores of the Lethe.*

### CHAPTER 2

# History and Enlightenment

## I  *The Living Brought to Judgment*

*A Vision on the Shores of the Lethe* is a satirical poem in which Batyushkov condensed a critical survey of Russian poetry from the time of Lomonosov to 1809. The lines devoted to contemporary literature ridicule the hostile camps of Admiral Shishkov and his followers, the "Shishkovites," and the emulators of Karamzin's Sentimentalism.

The attack against the "Karamzinites" constitutes but one brief episode in Batyushkov's poem. Its originality lies in its scope of contemporary poetry and in the creation of a panoramic picture of what the young poet disliked and what he felt he should oppose. Not only is the Sentimental poet Shalikov satirically portrayed, but also the eclectics, Merzlyakov and Yazykov (an ex-colleague of Batyushkov at the Ministry of Public Education); not only Shishkov and his fellow members of the Russian Academy, but the poet Semyon Bobrov, whose ideas were in many ways similar to those of the Shishkovites; Sergey Glinka, the editor of the reactionary journal *The Russian Messenger (Russky vestnik),* various women poets and, finally, the fabulist, Ivan Krylov, all were satirized in the poem.

Russian literary satire had not known such a variety of portraits before Batyushkov. No one before him had undertaken this bold a critical assessment of almost all the movements of contemporary literature. Batyushkov applied the technique of literary satire so often used by French poets of the eighteenth century. He depicted an infernal Judgment Day over dead poets, or over living poets declared dead for the purposes of the poem, a Judgment which convention dictated should be conducted by the shades of great writers long since departed. Batyushkov's poem is closest in satirical theme and subject to Alexis Piron's *Danchet aux Champs-Elysées* and Jean-François de La Harpe's *L'ombre de Duclos.* In Piron's poem, Danchet, a deceased translator of Virgil, finds himself in

Hades where he meets the gods of the underworld and the shades of dead French and Roman writers including Horace, Ovid, and Cicero. The poem ridicules the French Academy, where new members are selected for their disposition rather than for their talent.

La Harpe's poem has much in common with Piron's, but adds the subterranean river Lethe in which all the writers must be immersed; the mediocrities are drowned, but the talented swim safely ashore.

Batyushkov harnessed some of the comic techniques of French literary satire to the general purpose of his poem: to combat literary opponents who, at the same time, opposed his views on the development of society. Written as a literary satire, Batyushkov's poem also turned out to be a serious statement against literary obscurantism and social reaction.

The main enemy against whom Batyushkov was tilting was the group of literary figures who, in 1807, had united around Shishkov rallying to the standard of extreme conservatism in politics and literature. The center of literary conservatism was the Russian Academy, of which Shishkov himself was an active member. By the time Batyushkov began writing his *Vision*, Shishkov had succeeded in gathering a large following and was conducting a determined struggle—not against Karamzin any longer, who since 1804 had been busy with history—but against all those in whose social or literary ideas he detected the least spark of originality.

The year *A Vision on the Shores of the Lethe* began to circulate, Shishkov's closest disciple and most talented follower S. A. Shikhmatov, came out with his *Hymn To the Russian Word (Pesn' rossiyskomu slovu)*[1] which, like Batyushkov's poem, was a critical evaluation of Russian poetry up to Shishkov's time. Shikhmatov's choice of names is characteristic of his literary affiliations. After praising Kantemir, Lomonosov, Sumarokov, Kheraskov, and particularly Derzhavin, Shikhmatov writes an enthusiastic eulogy of Shishkov and other members of the Russian Academy. He makes absolutely no mention of Bogdanovich, Karamzin, or Dmitriev, that is, those writers whom Batyushkov considers as founders of a new epoch. Batyushkov, in his *Vision*, treats the acknowledged authorities of Russian literature of the eighteenth century and of the pre-Karamzin period with every appearance of respect. He does not allow himself to make fun of them in any way except for a passing dig at Trediakovsky.* All other writers are depicted in the light, bantering tone which distinguishes the poem as a whole:

> . . . pochtenny *Lomonosov*
> *Kheraskov,* chest' i slava rossov,
> *Samolyubivy Febov syn.*
> *Nasmeshnik, grozny bich porokov,*
> Zamyslovaty *Sumarokov*
> *I,* Mel' pomeny drug, *Knyazhnin*
>
> . . . . . . . . . . . . . .
> *I ty tam byl, naezdnik khily*
> *Stroptiva devstvennits sedla,*
> *Trudolyubivy, kak pchela,*
> Otets stikhov "Tilemakhidy."[2]

> . . . and *worthy* Lomonosov
> Kheráskov, *glory of the Russ,*
> Proud son of Phoebus, great in self-esteem.
> Dread scourge of vice and sharp-tongued mocker
> *Obscure and complex* Sumarokov
> And *Melpomene's friend,* Knyazhnin.
>
> . . . . . . . . . . . . . . . . . . . . . . . .
> You, too, were there, uncertainly bestriding
> The unbroken saddle of virginity,
> Hard-working hack, as busy as a bee,
> Your "Telemachus" on his journeys guiding.

Thus, the *Vision* does not directly criticize nor openly cast down the literary idols of the past, although the familiar tone in which Batyushkov writes of them amounted to challenging the official, conservative camp in literature.

Batyushkov's flippancy and lack of proper respect for accepted authorities was emphasized by the warm sincerity of the lines in honor of Khemnitser:

> *I ty, o moy pevets nezlobny,*
> *Khemnitser, v basnyakh bespodobny!*[3]

> And you, mild bard, incomparable
> Khemnitser, master of the fable

And particularly by his enthusiastic praise of Bogdanovich:

> *I ty sidel v tolpe izbrannoy,*
> *Stydlivoy gratsiey venchannoy,*
> *Pevets prelestnyya mechty,*
> *Mezhdu Psikhei legkokryloy*

---

*The translator of Fénelon's *Télémaque.*

*I boga nezhnoy krasoty . . .*[4]

You, too, were here among the elect
By bashful Graces wreath-bedecked,
Wrapt poet, dreaming dreams of bliss,
Between the light-winged Psyche sat
And the fair God of tenderness.

From among the living "classics," Shikhmatov had singled out Derzhavin for particularly lengthy accolades. Batyushkov, on the contrary, preserved a diplomatic silence about the grand old man of literary conservatism, but subjected Shishkov's followers to the most merciless ridicule.

Shikhmatov, in his poem, hails Shishkov as a great mover of Russian literature.[5] He is equally enthusiastic in his praises of the other members of the Russian Academy, whom he apostrophizes as

Masters of rhetoric! Minstrels grandiloquent!
I thirst to sing your praise. But—ah!—my talent faints
My grateful lyre and lips lack eloquence[6]

. . . . . . . . . . . . . . . . . . . . . . . . . . . . . . . . .

In the *Vision*, Shishkov is made to say of Shikhmatov:

My youthful fellow-members here,
The love of Fame within them burning,
Of Prince Pozharsky they all sing,
And Hermogenes, the elder, they are drowning:
From Holy Writ they take their wording,
Their thoughts for Heaven take wing.[7]

Batyushkov is here alluding to Shikhmatov's lyrical poem *Pozharsky, Minin, Hermogenes or Russia Delivered* (*Pozharsky, Minin, Germogen ili spasennaya Rossiya*, 1807). The events described in this poem involve the expulsion of the Polish interventionists from Moscow in 1612, made possible thanks to the direct participation of God and His angels. The heroes' monologues, full of lofty pathos, are permeated with pious monarchism. Prince Pozharsky, one of the commanders of the people's volunteers, earns Shikhmatov's approval not so much because Russian troops defeated the Poles and liberated Moscow under his leadership, but because he refused the crown offered to him by a grateful people. Shikhmatov had used historical events to point out the analogy with Napoleon, hatred for whom had grown even stronger in monarchist circles throughout Europe since he had declared himself Emperor of France, thereby usurping—at least in the opinion of Emperor Alexander I and most of the Russian nobility—the lawful power of the French kings. Shikhmatov's poem concluded with an exhortation to the people of Russia to be true to the Tsar, the Faith and the Old Customs, and to oppose "infection" from abroad, that is, the ideas of the Enlightenment and the French Revolution:

> Oh Russ! Most blest among the nations:
> In heroism and piety
> Unmatched, unique in all creation!
> Incline thine ear to my fond plea:
> See ancient customs thrive in strength,
> Hold fast thy fathers' faith and be
> Its jealous guardian, verily!
> Reject all foreign countries' poisons
> Esteem your splendid native tongue,
> Be ardent for the Tsar, the Savior,
> Be Russian! And thus, great for ever,
> The powers of Hell shall't thou o'ercome.[8]

This passage from Shikhmatov's poem is a sufficient example of the kind of ideology and style which Batyushkov opposed in the poetry of his day. A number of archaic lexical forms used by Shikhmatov were totally unacceptable to Batyushkov, although only two years before the *Vision*, in his translation from Tasso, he himself had kept to the old high language, albeit without excessive use of Slavonicisms.

## II  *Literature and Politics*

The appearance of Shishkov and his followers on "the shores of the Lethe" is pure burlesque:

> *No vdrug na adskiy bereg dikiy*
> *Prizrak chudesnyy i velikiy*
> *V obshirnom dedovskom vozke*
> *Tikhon'ko tyanetsya k reke.*
> *Namesto klyachey zapryazhenny*
> *Tam lyudi v khomuty vlozhenny*
> *I tyanut koe-kak, guzhom!*[9]

> But suddenly to these wild shores of Hades
> A wonderful and mighty apparition is
> Toward the river wending his slow way
> Laied out on an ancestral sleigh.
> Instead of harnessed nags to draw him
> There are people yoked to haul him
> And barely can they pull the cart their way!

Batyushkov refrains from drowning Shishkov himself in the Lethe, but shows how Trediakovsky recognizes in him his true spiritual heir:

> Then glanced up with a fleeting leer
> The bard of amorous rides lubricious
> And spake: "O man of mind judicious
> To have found things both wise and fair
> In my poor *Diedamiya* here.[10]
> [*Diedamiya*—a tragedy by V. Trediakovsky.]

All the other writers who figure in the poem at this point Batyushkov drowns in the waters of Lethe, thereby proclaiming the uselessness and insignificance of their work. Batyushkov must have had a firm confidence in the justice of his own literary opinions and the prescience of his social attitudes to have committed himself to so drastic a critique of contemporary literature.

It should be noted that of all living poets the only one whom Batyushkov introduces with good will and real affection is Krylov, who had become a classic in his own lifetime. It is even possible that the compelling reason for Batyushkov's undertaking his *A Vision on the Shores of the Lethe* was the refusal of the Academy (on March 13, 1809, by 13 votes to 2) to elect Krylov to its membership, a circumstance which had greatly incensed the younger poet. In a letter from Gnedich to Batyushkov, we have an eyewitness account of Krylov's reaction to the *Vision*:

What a surprise it was for Krylov; he returned the other day from a gambling journey; that very same hour he was at Olenin's and was listening to the sentences pronounced by the snub-nosed judge* upon all the characters; he sat [as if] in the true image of one of the dead, and suddenly the whole edifice was shaken; there were tears in his eyes: I must confess, the whole performance might have been written for him alone.[11]

---

*i.e., Minos, supreme judge in the realm of the shades.

Dealing ruthlessly with nearly all contemporary writers, Batyushkov gave Krylov alone high praise.

The impression made by the poem on the writers ridiculed in it was only partially reflected in Gnedich's correspondence with Batyushkov. The young poet was extremely interested to hear all his friend had to tell him on this subject: "Tell me, has Shishkov read it?... Well, are they cursing me? Who and how? Write me a full description, keeping nothing back."[12] On February 19, 1810, Gnedich informed him: "At last the Slavophiles have read *Lethe* —and who do you think is the most enraged?—Derzhavin."[13] Some time later an apprehensive and hurt Batyushkov was writing to him of his meeting with an acquaintance:

Yesterday I saw Ermolaev... he said that there's a storm building up against me in your parts. Not only that: I am held to be to blame. You know best whether I wanted to publish abroad a trifle, in fact written as a joke for my own circle of friends. However, the more they scold, the more it will prick them, and that is a true sign in the teeth of the judges that it is even well written... it will be a long, a very long exile from Parnassus, where I see nothing but asses. They say the bard of Felitsa and *Vasily the Black* [i.e., Derzhavin] is arming himself still more heavily! Help!... Say who will that our literature is flourishing... I often put myself in the place of the people who have succeeded in swimming across the Lethe. Should I be angry? No, truly, no and no!... My comfort is this: the storm will die down and then they will realize the truth of my words. My dream will come bobbing up to the surface again, I am sure...[14]

A week later, Batyushkov had not merely shaken off his apprehension but was feeling confirmed in the rightness of his judgments after reading a new poem by Shikhmatov, *Peter the Great* (1810):

Send me a detailed description of the rage of these feeble riders of the Slavonic Pegasus. By the way, I may tell you that Ermolaev arrived here in despair and anger... arrived and foretold that I was about to run into rough weather on your Pindus, Helicon, and Parnassus; he spilled out a whole tankful of malice and I, and I—well, I went and believed him, got thoroughly upset and even went so far as to lose a few nights' sleep in contemplation of the havoc I had wrought.... Now I see that it was nothing but a tempest in a tea cup...[15]

And further, arguing with Gnedich who had evidently referred to the *Vision* ... as "agreeable nonsense," Batyushkov gives his evaluation of it, an evaluation which is all the more noteworthy because, even at this point in time, it would be difficult to add to it or improve on it: "It will live on ... not as something perfect in itself, but as an original and amusing work, a work in which a man without the least respect for personality has judged justly between talent and twaddle."[16]

Batyushkov looked on his *Vision* ... as a public declaration, which, in the context of the literary struggle of those years, it truly was.

The literary attack against the emulators of Karamzin was secondary to the attacks against the champions of social and literary reaction. Shishkov and his followers considered the "new style,"—the school of Karamzin in prose and poetry—to be a direct reflection "of the ideas and spirit of the monstrous French Revolution." Consequently, they advocated a literature based on the traditions of the eighteenth century classics (Kantemir, Lomonosov, Sumarokov, Derzhavin), with its strict division between the high and the low, and its all-pervading monarchism, conservatism, and patriotism.

In 1808 the polemics between Shishkov and his opponents flared up with a renewed virulence. Shishkov had published a pamphlet entitled *A Translation of Two Articles from La Harpe"* (*Perevod dvukh statey iz Lagarpa*), in the introduction to which he had written:

When the monstrous French Revolution, having laid low everything that was founded in the laws of faith, honor, and reason, proceeded to produce in their country a new language very different from the language of Fénelon and Racine, then our literature, modeling itself on their new literature and on the German, disfigured by French nomenclature, began to lose all resemblance to the Russian language.[17]

In the same year, Sergey Glinka began to publish his journal *The Russian Messenger* (*Russky Vestnik*), devoted entirely to the defense of Russian culture, customs, and traditions from the pernicious influence of all things foreign, particularly French eighteenth century Enlightenment and arguments of materialist thinkers and atheists.

On the one hand, Glinka idealized pre-Petrine Russia, while on the other he subjected to fierce criticism the thinkers of the Enlightenment: "The Boyar Matveev meditated on the soul no less than Locke and Condillac, although he could not have read either. True enlightenment is distinguished by clarity and simplicity of concepts, false teaching by confusion and arrogance."[18]

The superiority of pre-Petrine Russian ways, according to Glinka, was that

while growing up in the fear of God and in simplicity of life, our ancestors acquired all their ideas from *the teachings of their fathers and from spiritual books*. They did not argue about some original natural state, about the infinite perfectibility of the human mind, but strove to fulfill their duties as men, citizens, and Christians.[19]

By thus praising the Russia of the olden days, Glinka mutely denied the inevitability and progressive quality of the reforms of Peter I.

These statements by the champions of the pre-Petrine past and patriarchal ignorance forced Batyushkov to clarify his social and literary positions in his own mind and made him an even more staunch supporter of the ideas of the Enlightenment. His patriotism was founded on love for his native land, illumined by a reasonable understanding of the true requirements for national development. When he sent Gnedich *A Vision on the Shores of the Lethe* he wrote to him as to a friend with similar ideas.

One should love one's fatherland. Whoever does not is a monster. But is it possible to love ignorance? Is it possible to love manners and customs from which we are separated by ages and, what is more, by the entire Age of Enlightenment? Why do these busy scribblers single out everything that is old for their praise? Believe me, though! These patriots, these ardent speech-makers do not love or do not know how to love the land of Russia. I have the right to speak, and it would be a good thing if everyone else who had been prepared voluntarily to sacrifice his life for his fatherland would speak his mind on this.[20]

## III *Peter I: Revolution or Reform?*

Not long before the beginning of the new war against Napoleon in 1811, Batyushkov wrote a satirical essay entitled *A Stroll through*

*Moscow* (*Progulka po Moskve*), in which he formulated his ideas
on contemporary social customs in the light of his own concept
of history. What attracted Batyushkov to Moscow was the harmonious fashion in which the city combined various ways of life:
the modern and enlightened with the old and patriarchal, which still
had something of the genuine flavor of pre-Petrine ways and customs. He compares the Kremlin with Kuznetsky Most, the most
fashionable shopping street in Moscow:

> Let us now enter the Kremlin. To right and left we see magnificent buildings
> and resplendent cupolas with high towers, and all this girdled by an im-
> pregnable wall. Here everything breathes of ancientry: everything recalls
> the Tsars, the Patriarchs, historical events, here every place bears the im-
> print of times gone by. Here everything is in contrast to what we see on
> the Kuznetsky Most, on Tverskaya Street, on the Boulevard, etc. There
> are French bookshops, fashion shops whose hideous advertisements hide
> the façades of entire buildings, watch-makers, wine-cellars and, in a word,
> all the paraphernalia of fashion and luxury.[21]

The contrasts between these pictures of Moscow life do not prevent
Batyushkov from seeing and appreciating the significance of Moscow
as the result of a nation's labors throughout the centuries, as a symbol of Russia itself.

*A Stroll Through Moscow* was written during a period of outwardly friendly relations between Russia and France, although
signs of a new, decisive conflict were already in evidence. For reasons
of censorship, Batyushkov could not refer to this directly, but he
gives his evaluation of the political future of Russia by means of
comparison with the German states which at that time were completely subjected to Napoleon:

> He who has stood in the Kremlin and looked unmoved upon the gigantic
> towers, the ancient monasteries, the magnificent view of the town across
> the river, and has not felt pride in his fatherland and has not called down
> blessings upon Russia, such a one (and I say this without hesitation) is a
> stranger to all greatness, because he has been piteously deprived by nature
> at his very birth. Let him go to Germany and live and die in some little
> town under the shadow of a parochial steeple together with the peaceable
> Germans who, immersed in petty political calculations, have voluntarily
> tendered wrists and ankles to be clamped in the irons of most horrible
> slavery.[22]

Belief in the historic destiny of Russia in the context of the contemporary political situation did not prevent Batyushkov from
clearly perceiving the variance of interests and opinions among the
Moscow nobility. He ridicules those who wish "to be taken for
foreigners, affect the French 'r' and put on airs," but neither does
he spare the indolence of the Muscovites: "Idleness is a common
feature, exclusively typical of this city . . . In Moscow people *rest,*
in other towns they are more or less engaged in work, and for this
reason in Moscow they are well acquainted with boredom and all
her torments."

As an oasis in this desert of idle curiosity and inertia which is
such a "spacious field for comic authors," Batyushkov distinguishes
a house which is "indwelt by hospitality, decorum, and sociability,"
whose inhabitants center their lives around the interests of the
present day rather than around the prejudices of their forefathers.
Batyushkov's picture of life in Moscow in many ways anticipates
Griboedov's comedy *Woe from Wit* (*Gore ot uma*), written some
ten years later,[23] with its portraits of Moscow eccentrics and its
satirical depiction of the manners of the city's nobility.

Batyushkov's essay combined satire of manners and customs
with a general assessment of the state of culture and enlightenment
of the Russian nobility of his time. Batyushkov appeared here as
a champion of true Enlightenment, which he considered the first
condition of social progress. Thus, in his *Stroll Through Moscow,*
Batyushkov formulated his opinion of Peter I and his reforms, an
opinion quite at odds with the idealization of pre-Petrine customs,
which at that time was cultivated by all representatives of conservative
ideology. Under the impression of the panorama of Moscow which
opened up before anyone looking from the ramparts of the Kremlin,
Batyushkov wrote:

A strange mixture of old and new architecture, of pauperism and wealth,
of European manners, and the manners and customs of the East! Wonderful,
unfathomable fusion of business and vanity with true glory and magnifi-
cence, ignorance with enlightenment, sociability with barbarity. Do not
be surprised, my friend: Moscow is the display sign or the living picture
of our fatherland. . . . And I, seeing the traces of times old and new, recalling the past and comparing it with the present, murmur quietly to myself: "Peter the Great accomplished much but finished little."[24]

Batyushkov's firm conviction that the task of Peter the Great must continue, and that literature and poetry should be called upon to play a role of great significance in reforming social customs, was expressed in his essay *An Evening with Kantemir (Vecher u Kantemira),* written in 1816.

Prior to that, however, in the essay *A Stroll Through the Academy of Arts* (*Progulka v Akademiyu Khudozhestv,* 1814), a subject which seems sufficiently far removed from contemporary social and political problems, Batyushkov again expressed his enthusiastically admiring attitude toward Peter I as the creator of Petersburg. He imagined Peter on first seeing the mouth of the Neva at the moment when the dream of building a new capital city was born in his mind:

My imagination showed me Peter, looking out for the first time over the banks of the desolate Neva, so beautiful now, in our day! From the *Nyunskant* fortress the Swedish cannon was still roaring; the delta of the Neva was still blockaded by the enemy and frequent bursts of gunfire were yet to be heard from the marshy banks when the great thought was born in the mind of the great man. There will be a city here, he said, one of the wonders of the world. I will summon all the arts here, all the crafts. Here the arts, the crafts, civil establishments, and laws will conquer Nature herself. So he spoke—and Petersburg arose from the desolate marshes.[25]

Kantemir attracted Batyushkov's attention both as a poet, the originator of modern Russian literature, and as a civic figure, a convinced supporter of the Petrine reforms. The basic content of *An Evening with Kantemir* is an imaginary dialogue on the future of Russia between Kantemir, the French social philosopher Montesquieu, and another acquaintance of his, the Abbot V. In Batyushkov's essay, Kantemir questions Montesquieu's assertion that climate has a decisive formative influence on a country's way of life and that, therefore, the severity of the Northern climate must have a baneful effect on the cultural development of Russia: "What power will alter climate?" asks Montesquieu. "Who can give you a new sky, new air, new soil?" And Abbot V., agreeing with Montesquieu, seeks to persuade Kantemir that the Petrine reforms will prove to be short-lived:

All the efforts of the Titanic Tsar, all that he has brought to be with his iron hand, all will fall back into ruin, collapse, disappear. Nature, ancient customs, superstition, incurable barbarity will gain the upper hand over the feeble and ill-founded Enlightenment, and all this semi-barbaric Muscovy will again become barbaric Muscovy, and the eternal mists of oblivion will cover the deeds and the lives of Peter's successors.[26]

Kantemir refutes his opponents, giving expression to Batyushkov's own most heartfelt convictions, his profound belief that social progress in Russia must go hand in hand with Enlightenment. What Kantemir says of the destiny of Russia is in fact Batyushkov's political program for his own time—for 1810 and the ensuing decade—an expression of his hopes for reform from above, which many representatives of the nobility's intelligentsia expected from Alexander I after the victorious conclusion of the War of 1812. "Time destroys and creates everything, corrupts, and perfects," says Batyushkov's Kantemir.

Perhaps in two or three centuries, perhaps sooner, the kind Heavens will give us a genius who will fully comprehend all of Peter's great thoughts, and then, the vastest country in the world, obedient to his creative voice, will establish itself as the repository of laws, of the freedom founded upon them, of a way of life which gives stability to these laws; in a word, as the repository of enlightenment.[27]

One of the pre-conditions for a flourishing of the Enlightenment in Russia was, Batyushkov considered, the development of literature, especially of poetry. For this reason, deliberately disregarding strict historical accuracy, Batyushkov makes his Kantemir prophesy, in the year 1740, the appearance of Lomonosov, Derzhavin, Karamzin, and Dmitriev:

Who knows? Perhaps on the wild banks of Kama or the majestic Volga great minds will arise, rare talents. What would you say, Monsieur le Président, if you were to hear that by the ice floes of the northernmost sea amidst the half-wild peoples there was born a great genius who strode like a Titan through all the fields of science as a philosopher, orator and poet, reformed his mother-tongue and left behind him indestructible monuments to his own labors?[28]

Batyushkov's position as a defender of progressive views had not changed since the publication of his *Vision on the Shores of the Lethe*. From 1809 to 1811 Batyushkov read and reread the French eighteenth-century philosophers of the Enlightenment, Voltaire, d'Alembert, d'Holbach, and others. Batyushkov himself was of deistic convictions and rejected the materialist atheism of d'Holbach which he refuted with arguments borrowed from Voltaire:

The author of *Système de la Nature* [d'Holbach] is like an artist who has mixed all his colors together and afterwards seems to be saying: "There, see if you can distinguish black from white now, or red from blue ..." At the end of his book, this same author, having pulled everything down and mixed everything up, calls in Nature and makes her the origin of all things. And so, dear friend, it is impossible for anyone to deny and not to discover some First Principle, call it what you may, it all comes to the same thing: but it exists, that is, God exists.[29]

In answer to a letter from Gnedich in which his friend advises him against spending too much time on the philosophers of the Enlightenment, Batyushkov wrote at the end of December 1809: "I laughed at the exhortation not to read Mirabeau, d'Alembert, and Diderot. Coming from Gnedich that is really funny! Since when did you join the Capucines?" Here Batyushkov is using the appellation "Capucine" in Voltaire's habitual sense as a synonym for hypocrite.

Batyushkov's attitude toward Voltaire did not change during the new war, although his attitude toward the French as a nation did. Voltaire, however, remained for him, as before, "the most worthy man of his age, wonderful, unique ... who knew everything, said everything, who had a kind, extraordinary heart, a subtle, far-ranging, brilliant mind, capable of anything and, finally, a character quite unlike what one would expect either from his mind or from his heart," wrote Batyushkov in 1814 in the essay *Journey to the Castle of Cirey* where, in the company of Mme du Châtelet, Voltaire had spent the best years of his life. *Journey to the Castle of Cirey,* like Batyushkov's other prose pieces, particularly his *Stroll Through Moscow,* is permeated with the pathos of historical change. Muscovite and post-Petrine Russia are contrasted throughout the *Stroll Through Moscow,* just as, in the *Journey to the Castle of Cirey,* "Time gone by," that is prerevolutionary France, is contrasted with the France of the Restoration.

In each case, the comparison of two epochs in the history of a nation had a specific purpose. In *Stroll Through Moscow,* Batyushkov contrasted ancient and modern times in order to prove the beneficence of reform and to convince his reader that only peaceable transitions and systematic enlightenment are able to bring lasting, workable results. In his *Journey to Cirey* Batyushkov expresses his views toward the French Revolution and its results, utilizing different literary devices. An old peasant whom he meets upon the road has this to say about the fate of France:

There's been more than one Revolution here, Monsieur l'Officier, more than one Revolution! I've lived through one in my lifetime: hard times . . . no better than now! We planted the Liberty Tree . . . I myself had the honor of planting it just over there, on the green meadow. . . . And the churches of the Lord were sacked. . . . I could not raise my hand to such evil! . . . But how did it all end? They cut down the tree and the writing on the wall of the Church porch, *liberty, fraternity or death,* has been white-washed over. What haven't I seen in my lifetime! Enemies on the soil of my motherland I've seen, and now here I am talking to a Cossack officer![30]

This same tale of the astonishing cycle of events which brought Russian troops into the heart of France is taken up by another character in the story, a Monsieur R-n, "an inhabitant of Cirey," who says of Voltaire: "He foresaw much, foretold much in politics; but could he have foreseen that a few decades later you would come to Emilia's castle carrying arms, together with a crowd of men from the Volga and people who drink the waters of Siberia . . ."[31]

This insistent comparison of "times past" with the present state of Europe—a comparison which is full of thoughts about the French Revolution, its results, the effect it will have on the future development of Europe—is the basic idea of the essay. The actual principle of comparing past and present was widespread among eighteenth-century thinkers, characteristic of the methodology of their historic meditations, and Batyushkov, by his adaptation of this method, appears in this sense as a faithful pupil of eighteenth-century Enlightenment.

There is, however, a real difference between the historic philosophy of Batyushkov and the historic conceptions of Montesquieu and Voltaire. The French thinkers had only had past revolutions to go by—nothing but theory. Batyushkov and his generation, however, had themselves experienced the greatest bourgeois revolution of all: he had grown up, attained maturity, and become an officer in the

Russian Army during wars born of the French Revolution and of its result—the dictatorship of Napoleon. By the time Batyushkov wrote his *Journey to Cirey*, it must have seemed to him that the time had come to draw some conclusions from an epoch which was now ended. The Revolution had become the object of his meditations, for its experiences and consequences were a direct and vital emotional experience of his own life and thought.

The thought inherited from the philosophers of the Enlightenment was already insufficient to explain the course of world destiny and, above all, to grasp the predestination of man, to point to his place in the world of history as an individual. That is why the theme of man, his potentialities, his limitations, and his ways to happiness became the basic content of Batyushkov's work after he had grown out of his dependence on literary models and found his own poetic manner.

CHAPTER 3

# In Quest of Individual Style

## I   Batyushkov and Derzhavin

*A* *Vision on the Shores of the Lethe* was not only a literary and political, but also a serious artistic achievement for a twenty-two-year-old poet. Surviving copies of the poem show how much time and thought he gave to the selection of final forms for the most important passages. In the first versions of some lines it is still obvious that Batyushkov wrote his poem with all the spontaneity and dash so characteristic of his letters to his friends, in which he was always ready with a bold, sometimes thoroughly risqué jest. In a letter to Gnedich written not long before the completion of the *Vision*, Batyushkov painted the following ironic picture:

From your letter I see that you are living in a *dacha* which is a habitation of sirens. Courage, Ulysses! Here, there is not one siren, but other companions of the man of Ithaca who took ten years to sail from Asia Minor to his rocky and poverty-stricken island... I opened the window and beheld: the dear little nymph Io wandering by, mooing, heaven knows what about; two Ledas gaggling mercilessly. And, look ... in the shade over there—indeed, I am ashamed to admit it!... sheep, possibly from the herd of King Admetus...[1]

Quite in the spirit of this jesting are the following lines written for the *Vision:*

> *Drugoy v Tsiteru prenesën,*
> *Poteya nad prekrasnoy nimfoy*
> *Khotel eë nasil'no—pet'!*[2]
> And one to Cythera transported
> Was struggling with a beauteous nymph
> And sweating to enforce—a lay!

In the final text these lines were replaced by others:

> *Drugoy v Tsiteru prenesën,*
> *Krasu, umil'nuyu kak Gebu,*
> *Khotel dlya nas nasil'no . . . pet'.*[3]
> And one to Cythera transported,

47

A beauty, mild and sweet as Hebe's,
For us was struggling to . . . lay!*

While avoiding word-for-word repetition of the joking verse interpolations in his letters, Batyushkov retained the same spontaneity and freedom which hitherto he had used only in verses for his friends. He does not hesitate to play the whole gamut of jokes, irony, and puns.

In his description of Sergey Glinka, he makes use of the pun:

*Dlya russkikh* prav *moy tolk* krivoy[4]

Can be read either:

For Russian rights my views are crooked

Or:

For Russians, my crooked views are right

From the words he puts into the mouth of Fonvizin, the proverb is given an ironic twist, reminiscent of its use in fables:

*"Aga!" Fonvizin molvil brat'yam—*
*"Zdes' budet vstrecha* ne po plat'yam,
*No po zaslugam i umu"*[5]

"Aha!" Fonvizin told his fellows:
"They won't be judged here by their tailors,
But on their merits and their minds."

In the spirit of the anticlerical satires of Voltaire and Parny, Batyushkov depicted the behavior of the corpulent bon vivant, Ivan Krylov, in Hell. Called before the Infernal judgment seat, the shade of Krylov gives this account of itself:

Death caught me unawares, poor sinner,
As I was sitting at my dinner:
But now I'm quite prepared to try
Once more with you the wine of Hades
And take a slice of Pluto's pie.[6]

---

* The Russian is more subtle, relying on the difference between the expected, unprintable verb without the "p" and the perfectly innocent "pet"—to sing.

This emancipation from the old wornout stylistic canons, taboos, and rules, as well as the freedom of poetic imagination and poetic vocabulary which Batyushkov demonstrates, was also a constructive program which inspired him and made his criticisms so forceful and his satire so fearless.

Batyushkov, having ridiculed bad and ungifted poets, was now faced with having to solve an even more difficult problem requiring all his talent, boldness, and resolution: he had to find his own poetic style in order to express his views on the principal literary theme of the time—the intimate world of the human heart and mind. Thus, while he was working on *A Vision on the Shores of the Lethe,* Batyushkov also read the poetry of his most diverse Russian contemporaries and worked on translations of such widely differing poets as Tibullus, the Roman elegist, Petrarch, the originator of the European love lyric, and his own contemporaries, Parny, the French elegist and Casti, the Italian satirical poet. At the same time he reread Derzhavin, voicing enthusiasm over his *Description of the Feast of Potemkin* (*Opisanie Potemkinskogo prazdnika*), and declared the verses of Kapnist a model of poetic style: "He who wants to write and to be read should write comprehensibly like Kapnist, the most reliable model for style,"[7] he wrote to Gnedich on September 19, 1809. These opinions expressed in the letters to Gnedich, together with the critical section of *A Vision on the Shores of the Lethe,* reflect the systematic reevaluation of the state of Russian poetry which, in Batyushkov's literary development, went hand in hand with the elaboration of his own poetic style.

At the beginning of the nineteenth century Russian poetry was represented by poets of various generations and various schools. The creators of Russian Sentimentalist poetry, Karamzin and, more especially, Dmitriev, had cultivated a lyric poetry of personal feeling in new, or rather renovated, poetic genres: the song, the fable, the epistle and, more rarely, the elegy. Batyushkov had grown up on Dmitriev's poetry; there is no other Russian poet whom he so readily quotes in his letters and articles. In Dmitriev's poetry it was the image of the poet himself which attracted young writers: the exquisite epicurean of his tales and elegies or the sly, witty raconteur of his fables.

The poetry of Kapnist which Batyushkov admired so greatly occupied an intermediate position between Dmitriev and Derzhavin.

Kapnist, who had begun to write under the influence of Derzhavin and introduced genuine biographical elements into his poetry, later, under the influence of Dmitriev, carefully eradicated all traces of biographical data and subordinated the entire sphere of his creative work to the image of the Sentimental poet, somewhat in the spirit of Horace.

Less straightforward was Batyushkov's attitude to Derzhavin. The supreme exponent of Russian Classicism, as a writer of odes, the heir to Lomonosov, Derzhavin's evolution had been as complex as that of the poetry of his age. Batyushkov's attitude toward Derzhavin's poetry was one of respect and often of profound enthusiasm, but he did not look upon him as his teacher.

It is characteristic that in 1816, when enumerating Russian love poets and Anacreontic poets in *A Discourse on the Influence of Light Verse on Language,* Batyushkov traces them back to Bogdanovich and Dmitriev. He mentions Derzhavin in quite another context, referring only to Derzhavin's interest in the genre, but not to the significance of his Anacreontic verse in the history of Russian poetry: "The heir to Lomonosov's lyre is Derzhavin, whose name alone must be pronounced with reverence by all true talent; Derzhavin is the inspired singer of higher truths and, in the winter of his days, loved to relax with the old man of Teos"[8] [i.e., Anacreon].

The diplomacy of this description is evident; Derzhavin's later experiments in Anacreontic poetry represent, from Batyushkov's point of view, not so much a milestone in Russian poetry as a fact of the poet's private life. In Dmitriev, however, Batyushkov finds a carefully thought out system of evaluations for his contribution to each separate genre:

Dmitriev's witty, inimitable tales in which poetry has for the first time beautified the conversational style of the best society; the epistles and other works of this poet, in which philosophy comes alive through unfading flowers of expression; his fables in which he competed with La Fontaine and often excelled him . . .[9]

It was not that Batyushkov preferred Dmitriev's talent to the great talent of Derzhavin—Batyushkov was incapable of such an error. It was that for his own poetry he found more of an affinity in the works of Dmitriev and the other poets he names in the *Discourse* than in the extraordinarily rich and varied poetic heritage of Derzhavin.

From the point of view of the poetic school to whose stylistic canons Batyushkov wholeheartedly subscribed in the years 1808–1809—the school of Karamzin and Dmitriev—certain verses of Derzhavin's, charming as they were, had grammatical carryovers in the middle of lines, which were not acceptable, overly complex grammatical errors, and awkward metaphors. The tenets of the Karamzinian school insisted upon observing precision and clarity as indispensable conditions for expressing the intimate world of individual feelings.

Derzhavin's poetic manner was suited to express one poetic personality—Derzhavin's own. This poetic manner could not be made to serve anyone else; it could not express that general feeling of life which Batyushkov shared with his contemporaries, men of a generation who had come to maturity amid the political changes and European wars of the beginning of the nineteenth century. For them, Derzhavin was a great poet, but a man of another epoch, like Voltaire, even though he was still alive and writing, and from time to time still came out with unexpected masterpieces.

Derzhavin completed the development of Russian Classicism. His transition from the ode to Anacreontic verses was accompanied by stylistic reform. Instead of making rigid distinctions between words of different provenance depending on poetic genre, Derzhavin ventured to mix various stylistic strata of the language in one and the same poem. In his odes, Derzhavin operated with "high" and "low" words and concepts remarkably freely, mixing the unmixable with unprecedented boldness, but he still retained the basic idea that the various styles required words of various derivation. Moreover, his artistic effects were often obtained by the deliberate juxtaposition of elements of various styles. It was from Derzhavin that Batyushkov learned the art of combining words hitherto considered unmixable in poetry. This "mixing of the unmixable" can be illustrated, for example by Batyushkov's line from the elegy *Convalescence* (*Vyzdorovlenie,* 1816):

> Izdokhi strastnye, i *sila milykh slov.*[10]
> And passionate sighs, and *the power of sweet words.*

In modern Russian the combination *sila milykh slov* seems perfectly natural. At the beginning of the nineteenth century, however, it must have required great boldness and complete confidence in his own sense of literary and historical fitness to put side by side and to link such a concept of "high" style as *sila* (power or might), a word belonging to the poetry of ode and epic, with *mily* (sweet or dear), an epithet typical of an elegy or song, that is, of intimate love poetry.

The word *mily* which in our days has more or less a neutral connotation and is not charged with any predetermined stylistic associations was, at the beginning of the nineteenth century, viewed with apprehension by various literary groups. In his *Discussion of the Old and New Style of the Russian Language* (1803), Shishkov was particularly severe in his condemnation of the system of transferred word usage introduced by Karamzin. In particular, he dwells in detail on the frequent metaphorical use by Karamzin and his school of the epithet *mily*. Shishkov was not opposed to the metaphorical use of this epithet as a general principle, but was against its audacious coupling with abstract concepts.

It is very proper to say: "a *dear* friend," "a *sweet* face;" on the contrary, it is very strange and barbarous to hear "*sweet* goddess," "*dear* hope of immortality!" However beautiful and significant a word may be, if we are constantly to repeat it and use it without the least discrimination, wherever it happens to crop up, as in the books of today they use the word *milaya*, it will cease to be an ornament of language and will become nothing but one more fashionable catchword.[11]

Batyushkov did not make up his mind all at once to use the epithet *mily* in the audacious and unexpected combination as he did in the elegy *Convalescence;* usually it was used as a form of address or definition in the customary language of the love poem: *mily sad* (dear garden), *podrugi milye* (sweet friends/fem./), *drugi milye* (dear friends/masc./).

Not until 1813, in the epistolary poem *To Dashkov,* in which Batyushkov expressed his sorrow and anger at the sight of Moscow laid to ruin by the French, did he use the epithet *mily* in a bold and unexpected, but for this very reason, highly expressive context:

> *Iz miloy rodiny izgnannykh*
> From their dear homeland driven out

It was still later that the epithet appeared in his poetry in combination with *sila* (power or might).

## II  Batyushkov and Tibullus

When Batyushkov came to weigh and evaluate contemporary poetry in order to select what he felt to be close to his own ethic and aesthetic aspirations, he did not accept the real, autobiographical quality of Derzhavin's poetry. Nor did he feel justified in making a poetic theme of his own life as—albeit in very different forms—his elder contemporary Zhukovsky had done, following Derzhavin's lead. In Zhukovsky's poetry everything became a reflection of the fate of the poet, every verse was transformed into a page of his lyrical diary. Thus, all that was foreign or translated, in Zhukovsky's works expressed the same basic mood. The dominant appeal of this poetry—all of which could be read as a reflection of the fate of the poet—was that of his unhappy, unrequited, and only love.

Batyushkov did not follow either Derzhavin or Zhukovsky. Of the verses written from 1809 to 1810, the poem *Recollections of 1807* (*Vospominaniya 1807 g.*) is based on real events from the actual life of the poet. All other verses are translations and adaptations. The fate of this poem—in fact the only frankly autobiographical work in all Batyushkov's poetry—is very characteristic. First printed in 1809, the poem embodied the poet's recollections of the Battle of Heilsberg in March 1807, where he had been severely wounded. It tells of the "peaceful family" which nursed the wounded Russian officer back to health and of the love between him and Emilia. The poem begins and ends with dreams, the final scene being the appearance of the spirit of the poet's beloved:

> *I ya, obmanuty mechtoy,*
> *V vostorge sladostnom k ney ruki prostirayu.*
> *Kasayus' riz ee . . . i ten' lish' obnimayu!* [12]

> And I, deceived by this my dream,
> Enraptured stretch my arms out to the vision,
> I touch her robe . . . and clasp an apparition only.

The theme of dreams, that is, of poetic imagination, brings this poem closer to what Batyushkov had been writing between 1802 and 1807 when dreaming—life in a world created by his poetic imagination—replaced all other sources of inspiration. For this reason, in the poem *Recollections of 1807,* the lyrical hero still finds dreams far more important and significant than reality. He describes his dreams on the fields of Heilsberg in more detail than his wound, and the real romance with Emilia inspires him no more than does her appearance in his dreams.

When the poem was reprinted in *Essays,* Batyushkov omitted most of it, leaving only forty-three lines, and rechristened it simply *Recollection.* After this reworking, the poem became an elegy with its chief theme the contrast between war and the peaceful life of "a quiet stay-at-home." The narrative of healing love was discarded; the only remaining autobiographical content was the story of the wound. The conflict between the material and the genre ended in the triumph of the genre. The narrative content of the happy but brief love of a wounded officer was ousted by material more suited to the usual circle of elegiac themes.

The attempt to construct an elegy on autobiographical foundations struck Batyushkov as unsuccessful. He was not attracted by the idea of composing poetry based on the interest of the events described, on individual biographical implications "between the lines." What he was looking for was a new technique for the verbal and poetical expression of a state of mind and of the heart. This was why, in the years 1809–10, Batyushkov turned to various poetical systems, to the poetry of various peoples, so that by comparing the voices of others, he might find his own. If we make a chronological examination of Batyushkov's translations we find that, against an average of two or three verse translations a year, he made ten such translations in the year 1810, of which six were from Parny, two from Petrarch, and two from Casti. To this we may add two elegies by Tibullus translated at the end of 1809. Between 1809 and 1810, Batyushkov was translating more than before and paying particular attention to Parny of whom, in his earlier translations, he had made a melancholy dreamer. This renewed interest in Parny, the translations from Tibullus, Petrarch, and Casti, all bear witness to Batyushkov's profound dissatisfaction with his own work and to his determined search for a new poetic form. Translations from Latin and Romance poets were also of particular importance to Batyushkov, because in the work of the poets of his choice, there were no problems such as those which were creating the passionate arguments in Russian poetry. The Latin elegies of Tibullus, the sonnets and canzoni of Petrarch, and Parny's elegies were all written in a settled, homogeneous literary medium, permitting a choice of words and concepts purely according to the requirements of style and not according to etymological characteristics rigidly determined by the doctrine of three styles. In translating Italian or French poets, Batyushkov could concentrate his efforts on conveying the homogeneous style which for them was not an individual, but a general national characteristic. When he turned to poetry of other nations, Batyushkov tried to study what had been done by his own predecessors, by Russian poets who before him had been interested in the French or Roman elegy. He paid particular attention to all that Dmitriev had accomplished in his field, from his translations of Tibullus and Parny to his imitations of Petrarch.

Tibullus had begun to attract the attention of Russian poets only since the end of the eighteenth century. Other Latin poets, Horace and Ovid in particular, had been frequently translated from about 1750 onwards, and an enduring tradition already existed as to their poetic interpretation. The interest in Tibullus was a reflection of the widening interest in the lyricism of individual feeling which, from the end of the eighteenth century, was thought to belong largely to the sphere of the elegy, a genre especially intended for individual expression.

In French literature, Tibullus was one of the most popular of the ancient Roman elegists from 1770 until almost the end of the century. Parny, on the occasion of his acceptance into the French Academy, spoke of Tibullus' elegies as models for their genre.

Russian poets at the end of the eighteenth and beginning of the nineteenth centuries found in Tibullus a contrasting combination of themes: war and love, glory and peaceful, inconspicuous idyllic existence.

Translations from Tibullus provided an opportunity to do away with the divisions of genre in practice by following one peculiar method, that of including the theme of love in the sphere of the loftiest themes and problems which had hitherto been exclusive to the ode and to tragedy. The foundation for this tradition of a "Russian" Tibullus was laid by Dmitriev in his poem *The Elegy: An Imitation of Tibullus* (1795). Batyushkov, in his treatment of Tibullus' elegies, is close not only to Dmitriev, but also to Parny.

In Parny's opinion, Tibullus and Propertius occupy a peculiar place among the love poets of antiquity:

"Anacréon, Catulle, Horace dans quelques-unes de ses odes, et surtout Ovide, *sont les chantres du plaisir:* Properce et Tibulle sont les poètes de l'amour, les modèles de l'élégie tendre et passionnée."[13] But, Propertius "...a peine à se renfermer dans les bornes du genre élégiaque: son imagination l'entraîne et l'égare. Il met trop souvent entre Cynthie et lui tous les Dieux et tous les héros de la Fable."[14]

Tibullus, less inspired and ardent, has no such shortcoming. He, Parny holds, comes nearest to the true ideal of the elegiac poet: "Tibulle... est plus profondément sensible, plus tendre, plus délicat: il s'intéresse davantage à son bonheur et à ses peines."[15]

This attitude to Tibullus was typical of French elegiac poets of the school of Parny. His most talented follower, Charles Millevoye, repeated Parny's general evaluation of Tibullus in his article "Sur l'élégie" and expressed the same preference for Tibullus over Propertius.[16] At the same time, Millevoye contended that the modern poet should not reproduce the exact forms and techniques of the Classical elegy. For this reason, Millevoye prefers the elegies of (Parny to the elegies of Bertin,[17] who was closer in following the techniques and phraseology of the Latin elegiac poets.

In one of Antoine Bertin's elegies there is a comparison between the masters of a *country* and the master of a *heart* which, in Millevoye's opinion, is so out of place in an elegy that Parny would never have had recourse to it.[18] This example of an unsuccessful simile, thought to be against the canons of elegiac style, was very characteristic of the conception of the elegy to which Batyushkov also subscribed.

Dmitriev had printed his "imitation" of Tibullus in 1795. In it he emphasized the contraposition of war and glory to peace, rustic retirement, and love. However, Dmitriev's "elegy" lacks the essential elegiac theme: it is closer to the idyll; everything is painted in joyful and optimistic colors. The description is strongly russified, there is no mention of anything not to be met with in an ordinary Russian village: of the whole description, nothing but the last two lines have anything to do with Tibullus. Details of everyday life and the sentiments of the characters helped make Dmitriev's adaptation of Tibullus' elegy a modern poem both in its emotional pitch and in its apprehension of life.

Batyushkov follows Dmitriev closely in his translations of Tibullus's elegies, sometimes even echoing whole lines from his predecessor. Thus Dmitriev's elegy has:

> *O Deliya! dusha dushi moey i drug.*[19]

> O Delia! soul of my soul and friend!

And Batyushkov in his first published version:

> *Tot krov, gde s'edinën dushi moey s dushoy.*[20]

> That roof, where my soul lives with her soul close united.

In *Essays* Batyushkov revised this line:

> *Pod koim sopryazhen lyubov'yu s toboy . . .*[21]

> Beneath which I am linked with you in love . . .

Following the style of Dmitriev's translation from Tibullus sometimes even word by word, Batyushkov yet manages to remain closer to the Latin original. But, he replaces the theme of modest, unpretentious obscurity by the theme of poverty. He intensifies the contrast between the wealth of those favored by Fame and the secluded life of which the poet dreams:

> *O bednosti molil, s toboyu razdelennoy!*
> *Molil, chtob smert' menya zastala pri tebe,*
> *Khot' nishcha, no s toboy . . .*[22]

> For poverty I prayed, that I might share with you!
> And prayed that death might find me at your side,
> Poor, maybe, yet together . . .

In Tibullus there is nothing in the least reminiscent of this theme of poverty; he simply writes of his desire to live with his beloved and to die in her arms. Further, the theme of poetry linked with love acquires, in Batyushkov's version, a certain social foundation and a broader significance as a comment upon social values.

Following the example of Dmitriev, Batyushkov introduced new themes into the elegy with even greater confidence; in his version the poet's position acquires a social significance. Now the poet is not simply a dreamer as in Batyushkov's early works, but is an opponent of the favorites of Fame and Glory—those rich careerist courtiers whose lives, for all their outward splendor and luxury, were devoid of beauty, love, and happiness.


### III    *Batyushkov and Petrarch*

In his translations from Petrarch, Batyushkov again had Dmitriev as a predecessor. In his *Imitations of Petrarch* (*Podrazhanii Petrarku,* 1797) Dmitriev had gone back to one of Petrarch's most characteristic themes, which was that an all-forgiving love animates all of nature and the world.

Batyushkov, in his translations-imitations of Petrarch, reestablishes the broader themes of his poetry. Together with the theme of love, he intensifies the theme of sorrow for his dead beloved. Apostrophizing Death, Batyushkov's poet (*On the Death of Laura; From Petrarch*) says:

> Before thee all is vain—both sorcery and power . . .
> Such is the will of fate! . . . Why, why should I live on?
> Alas! Each night again to weep away the hours
> And shed eternal tears upon responsive stone.[23]

Batyushkov is trying to convey the strength of feeling, in this case, the whole strength, all the immeasurability of sorrow for his dead beloved, not by description nor by the lyrical hero's own account of his feelings, but by conveying his physical condition, vividly expressive of the shock to his spirits. According to the Italian scholar, Nice Contieri, Petrarch's sonnet is transformed in Batyushkov's translation-adaptation into a sentimental romantic poem with nocturnal and sepulchral motifs quite alien to Petrarch.[24] He offers a similar interpretation for Batyushkov's translation of Petrarch's fourth canzone *Nel dolce tempo de la prima etade,* called *Evening* (*Vecher*) by the Russian poet, in which the image of the living stone (vivo sasso), a complex metaphor typical of Petrarch, is replaced by that of sepulchral granite.[25]

> And cypress groves, and hills all sleeping sound.
> Where I, at dead of night, poor son of sorrow.
> Knelt by the granite grave, oppressed, in awe profound.[26]

This kind of adaptation from Petrarch was, however, the result of a conscious desire to find new possibilities in Russian poetry for expressing the individual character of love and not, as Contieri has assumed, the result of a mistaken reading of the Italian original.

If we are to compare the chronologically close translations from Tibullus, Petrarch, and Parny—all made between late 1809 and 1810—it becomes evident that all were a part of one general exercise, the object of which was to work out a poetic style capable of expressing a new content and a spirit of the new age. After this work Batyushkov came to the conclusion that the basic rule of poetry was: "Live as you write and write as you live,"[27] and he went on to quote examples from the lives of poets to support his conception of the tie between a poet's life and work:

Let us take a look at the lives of some of those poets whose names are so dear to our hearts. Horace, Catullus, and Ovid lived as they wrote. Tibullus deceived neither himself nor others when he told his patron Messala that he would find joy neither in triumphs nor in the splendor of Rome, but in the tranquility of the fields, the healthy air of the forests, the gentle meadows, the stream which flowed past his home, and that little cottage with the simple straw thatch—the tumble-down cottage where Delia awaited him, her loosened hair tumbling over her high breasts... Bogdanovich lived in the world of fantasy he himself created when his hand drew for us the enchanting image of "Dushenka." Derzhavin on the wild banks of the Suna, sprayed by its boiling foam, sang the *Waterfall* and *God* in prophetic frenzy. And in our days, more rich in glorious deeds than favorable to the Muses, Zhukovsky, gifted with an ardent imagination and a rare ability to convey to others the profound feelings of a strong and noble soul—in the camp of warriors, to the roar of cannon, gazing at the glowing sky above his burning capital, wrote inspired verses, full of fire, movement, and power...[28]

In accordance with his idea that the life of a poet is mirrored directly in his work, Batyushkov elaborated his own concept of a poetic style, which he formulated in his letters to Gnedich, at the same time giving his opinions on the merits and shortcomings of the works of his contemporaries.

Correct, natural style—or, as Batyushkov preferred to call it, using the Russian word, "slog" ("manner of writing," "implementation of language")—is developed not in academies or congresses of scholars, but among educated members of society living in accordance with contemporary ideas and the vital interests of their time. Batyushkov attributed the flowering of Russian literature in the last quarter of the eighteenth century to the development of society as a whole: "The majority of the writers I have mentioned by name," he said in his *Discourse on the Influence of Light Verse* . . . ,

spent their lives among the society of the age of Catherine, so favorable to the sciences and to literature. It was there they acquired that sociability and polish, that good breeding, the reflection of which we find in their works; in the best society they learned to guess at the secret play of passions, to observe manners, to maintain all the conditions and relationships proper to polite society, and to converse intelligibly, lightly, and agreeably.[29]

These words reflected Batyushkov's new attitude toward the best society and the literary and political salon, similar to that advanced by Madame de Staël in her book *De la littérature, considérée dans ses rapports avec les institutions sociales* (1800). Her idea was that the true laboratory of literature and language would now pass from the aristocratic salons of pre-Revolutionary France to the democratized salons of Republican France, and would be revived on a new basis of equality in which only brain and talent and not merely title or rank would decide a person's importance.[30]

The stylistic standards which Batyushkov required of poetry were elaborated in letters to his literary friends. Lucidity is only one of the basic stylistic requirements on which he began to insist beginning in 1809. In a letter to Gnedich he defines these requirements: "Lucidity, fluency, precision, poetry, and . . . and . . . and . . . as few Slavonic words as possible."

His two fundamental stylistic requirements—lucidity and precision—had a particular significance.

By precision Batyushkov and his poet friends had in mind a negative concept: the absence of all obscurity, confusion, avoidable intricacy of expression and phraseology. Gnedich, criticizing one of Batyushkov's poems *The Warriors' Dream* (*Son Ratnikov*), wrote: "How am I expected to understand how the sword slides over the wetness of the waters? And what *is* the wetness? The water is wet—or wetness is a property of watery matter; worse than useless in poetry."[31] Gnedich was referring to the second part of the verse where, in the song of *Unhappy Erica*, every four lines end with the refrain:

> *Moy mech skol'zit po vlage vod!*[32]
> My sword slides over the wetness of the waters!

Batyushkov concurred with this criticism, saying: "Of course, *the wetness of the waters* is nonsense,"[33] and later, when he reprinted *The Warriors' Dream* under the title *The Soldiers' Dream* (*Son voinov*), Batyushkov discarded the five verses bearing this refrain. In this instance Batyushkov had sacrificed precision to fluency, to the euphony of the line. *Wetness* is the inevitable and inalienable property of water. From the point of view of poetic precision one may have either one or the other—*wetness* or *water,* but not their metonymical combination. In the given example it is the tautology which offends the principle of precision.

Lucidity was the most traditional demand made of poetic style; lucidity was required by Sumarokov in his disputes with Lomonosov; and lucidity was named by Voltaire as one of the fundamental canons of style: "Trois choses sont absolument nécessaires: régularité, clarté, élégance."[34]

In criticizing his friends' verses, Batyushkov's first requirement was lucidity. Having received from Gnedich his translation of Book IX of the *Iliad,* Batyushkov wrote:

I must tell you that I found many mistakes in language and in the accentuation of words: important mistakes which you ought to correct. I still find a great many Slavonic words which are quite out of place. They are fine in descriptive passages when the poet is speaking, but not good at all in the mouths of the heroes: they cool down the narrative and render outlandish that which *should be clear.*[35]

The concept of lucidity was no simple repetition of what Sumarokov and Voltaire had written before. Batyushkov's concept of lucidity is connected with his other stylistic requirements, and exists not independently, but as part of a definite system, the basis of which was established in the process of work on his translations-adaptations of 1809–1810.

## IV  *Parny's Influence*

The way in which Batyushkov solved the problem of style and language can be traced through his translations of 1810 to his verse adaptations of Parny's prose (*Chansons Madécasses* and *Le Torrent, Idylle Persane*). In his translation of the *Chansons Madécasses* Batyushkov had a forerunner in Dmitriev, who, in 1810, had printed his own verse translation of the sixth song, written in the form of a dialogue between Ampanani, the king of the tribe, and his prisoner Vaïna. Ampanani declares his love for Vaïna, but, on discovering she loves another, he releases her to go and search for her beloved.

Dmitriev translated the *Chansons Madécasses* into Alexandrine verse. He contributed to the style an elegant wit, characteristic of all his poetry. The first two lines of the "translation" have nothing whatever to do with Parny:

> Do not, fair captive maid, curse these wars,
> Forget your home: Not you my captive are, but rather I am yours.[36]

*Amant* (lover)—Dmitriev replaces by the stylistic euphemism *drug* (friend). To Vaïna's words: "O roi prends pitié des pleurs qui mouillent tes pieds!" is added a reply on behalf of the king which again is not to be found in Parny's original:

> *Vaïna*
> Behold, Oh King, my tears.
> *Ampanani*
>    *They are most precious to me.*
> What would you say by them, oh *beauty most divine?*[37]

Dmitriev did not only make a Russian poem of *Chansons Madécasses,* he "translated" it into a different stylistic system, recreating it in the likeness of his own elegies and songs, lending it the stylistic tone characteristic of the poetry of Sentimentalism.

Batyushkov translated Parny's *Song VIII* of *Chansons Madécasses* in verse, as Dmitriev had the sixth, but in iambic lines of four, not six feet. Stylistically, his translation inclines neither toward the elegy nor the love lyric of what may be called the usual European type. Parny had collected his songs of Madagascar, as we are informed in the notes to the *Collected Works,* on his travels about the island. "They breathe that simplicity and freedom which is born of Nature alone."[38]

The *Chansons Madécasses* were thus considered both by Parny himself and by his contemporaries as yet another of those reproductions of the poetic culture of primitive peoples which had flooded European literature at the end of the eighteenth—beginning of the nineteenth century.

The song which Batyushkov translated must have appeared especially interesting to him, as it reflected an aspect of local custom which had particularly astonished European readers, an aspect of which Parny had written: "The Madagascans are merry by nature. The men live in idleness while the women work." Batyushkov's translation is the monologue of a man, the chief of his tribe, who loves to watch his womenfolk dance and to listen to their songs.

Batyushkov saw the Madagascan poetry as a phenomenon of Oriental culture. This explains why he made his translations in a manner canonized in Russian poetry by Trediakovsky and Lomonosov for reproducing the lexical style of the Psalms and the Books of the Prophets of the Old Testament:

> *Vospoyte pesni mne devitsy*
> *Pletushchey seti dlya koshnits,*
> *Ili kak,* sidya u pshenitsy,
> Ona pugaet zhadnykh ptits.[39]

> Come, maidens, sing me pretty ditties
> As you weave *nets* for new-mown hay,
> Or, as *beside the wheatfields sitting,*
> You scare the greedy birds away.

The original had not wheat, but rice. Batyushkov's maiden is weaving nets for a *koshnitsa,* a kind of open-work bag for carrying newly mown hay; Parny's "jeune fille" is braiding her hair. In the last line Batyushkov has:

> *I nas u kushchi ozhidaet*
> *Postel' iz list'ev i pokoy.*[40]

> And where my tents are spread awaits us
> A bed of cool leaves and repose.

In the original these lines strike a more laconic and practical note: "Allez, et préparez le repas."

Besides the words "koshnitsa" and "kushcha" (in the sense of pavilion or tent) Batyushkov deliberately introduced entire

Biblical phrases: "Tsar' vozveselite slukh" (Rejoice the ear of the King) "No vetr vecherniy povevaet" (But the evening wind bloweth).

In exactly the same way Parny's *Le Torrent, Idylle Persane,* (*Istochnik*), received an additional dose of "Oriental" coloring. Batyushkov added such purely arbitrary lines as:

> ... for the innocent maiden
> Roses bloom here in the shade of the palm

> And the turtle dove even
> With his amorous mistress must envy our lot.[41]

Parny's brief and unemotional phrase *"j'y suis seul avec toi, près de toi,"* Batyushkov replaced by the more emotional and, according to his ideas, more "Oriental": "Sweet are the hours spent with thee in the desert lands."[42]

Apart from this intensification of the Oriental coloring, Batyushkov put the whole song into the first person, writing in the name of the lyrical persona (the chief), whereas Parny punctuated his character's monologue by authorial asides and comments. Batyushkov's purpose was to lend his poem unity of tone, to extend the "Oriental coloring" throughout the entire text and not to disturb the atmosphere by the author's explications.

## V  The Expression of Feelings

Unity of tone and stylistic structure was the aim Batyushkov set for himself throughout the years 1809 and 1810. His attempt at Oriental stylization was only one particular instance of this more general work. However, the unity of tone or, as Batyushkov and his contemporaries put it, the unity of language (*slog*) was, in turn, a particular problem subordinate to the general pathos of his poetry. His desire was to express, through poetry, in words, the inner content of human personality—the mind and heart of the individual. Batyushkov was a man of his time and a poet of contemporary life, but in his approach to that life he went his own, separate way. Batyushkov was not interested in simply writing verses on the ideas of the Enlightenment or on popular maxims, although such poetry was liked both by his poet friends and members of the "Free Society." Batyushkov believed that the national culture of each people is most completely expressed by its poetry, since poetry of all the arts is closest to man's soul and to his heart.

His rejection of the *grand genre* and the ambition to create epic poetry—albeit in translation, as his friend Gnedich had done—was the cause of a sharp disagreement between them. Gnedich wrote to Batyushkov on October 16, 1810, after reading his translations from Parny: "Your Persian Idyll and the other pieces printed with it . . . equally convey nothing beyond the fact that you have an excellent talent for poetry; but the subjects are unworthy of you."[43] Evidently, Gnedich had in mind poetry translations from Giambattista Casti, Petrarch, and Parny. In this same letter, Gnedich voices a general objection to Parny's verse and, for this reason, condemns Batyushkov's translation.

Batyushkov's interest in Evariste Parny was the result of a definite attitude against literary and political reaction, against the mystical literature and the mystical moods which at that time were being energetically spread through Russian society in connection with the revival of interest in Russian Freemasonry. Parny with his fresh light verse must have been especially attractive to Batyushkov at this time. The heir to the irreverent, blasphemous lines in Voltaire's works, author of *La Guerre des Dieux* (1799), *Le Paradis Perdu* (1805), *Les Galanteries de la Bible* (1807), Parny was also the creator of elegiac lyrical verse which was, both in mood and content, something quite new to French literature.

The poetic expression of love, earthly love devoid of any admixture of mysticism, intoxication with the delights of this earthly life, "the inspired apology for elegant sensuality" as Belinsky called it— this is what made Parny's poetry so attractive to Batyushkov and some other Russian poets of the second decade of the nineteenth century. His contemporaries, having witnessed the success of Parny's collections of poetry, the first of which, *Poésies érotiques,* had appeared in 1778, believed that the elegist had made an original contribution to French poetry and had completely obscured the authors of drawing-room epigrams and madrigals. Parny's depiction of "le véritable amour" in place of chocolate-box sentiments and pastoral passions attracted Russian poets of the early nineteenth century. In the 1830's, roughing out a plan for the development of Russian poetry, Pushkin mentioned the importance of French lyrics for Russian poetry and, in the plan for his long article that was to remain largely unwritten, he made a special point of emphasizing "Parny and the influence of sensualist poetry on Batyushkov, Vyazemsky, Davydov, Pushkin, and Baratynsky."[44] The list does not include Zhukovsky, although we know that he, also, translated Parny and that, indeed, his translation preceded Batyushkov's. Batyushkov was attracted from the beginning by Parny's "elegant eroticism"—Zhukovsky by his elegiac moods.

Batyushkov was on the look-out for different themes and motifs in Parny's work; he needed a model, an example, to help him recreate quite a different circle of poetic concepts of life. He was drawn by the other aspect of Parny's work which was why, in extremely free translations and sometimes in frank variations on the themes of the French elegist, he not only gave expression to his own poetic sensitivity, but actually entered into a direct literary polemic with Zhukovsky.

Batyushkov translated Parny's poem *La frayeur* comparatively faithfully; he omitted only the reference to the mother of the heroine. He also alters the description of the protection which Morpheus, the god of sleep, accords the lovers at the request of Cupid and in place of that description Batyushkov gives us the hero directly addressing his beloved:

> *Nam li vedat', Khloya, strakh!*
> *Gimeney za vsë ruchalsya,*
> *I amury na chasakh.*
> *Vsye v bezmolvii glubokom,*
> *Vsye pochilo sladkim snom!*
> *Dremlet Argus tomnym okom*
> *Pod Morfeyevym krylom!"*[45]

> Chloe, fear no midnight knock!
> Hymen has us in safe-keeping
> And the cupids on the clock.
> All the household sweetly dozes,
> All is plunged in silence deep.
> Morpheus' curving wing encloses
> Argus in a charméd sleep.

Thus, instead of the clever trick played by Cupid in alliance with Morpheus that we have in Parny's story, Batyushkov transforms the story of action into a static picture of nocturnal peace favorable to the lovers, lifting a quotation from the verses of his uncle Mikhail Muraviev *To the Goddess of the Neva* (*Bogine Nevy*, 1794)—with which he was certainly familiar: "I amury na chasakh" ("And the Cupids on the clock").[46]

Wherever he could, Batyushkov replaces Parny's descriptive and periphrastic digressions by direct and precise definition, his meditations and descriptions by action. In Batyushkov's version this action is not according to the abstract formulas of the love lyric, but is a dynamic movement, an unfolding of events.

The Cupids who watch over the lovers make their first appearance at the beginning of the poem. It is, therefore, entirely natural that they should continue to help them and take part in their nocturnal escapade:

> *Pomnish' li*, moy drug bestsenny!
> Kak s amurami tishkom,
> *Mrakom nochi okruzhenny*
> *Ya k tebe prokralsya v dom?*[47]

> Dearest love, do you remember!
> How with the cupids on the quiet,
> Dark-enshrouded, to your chamber
> I stole through your still house one night?

Whereas Parny has:

> *Te souvient-il ma charmante maîtresse,*
> *De cette nuit où mon heureuse adresse*
> *Trompa l'Argus qui garde tes appas?*
> *Furtivement j'arrivai dans tes bras.*[48]

Batyushkov deliberately introduces into the text of his "imitation," conversational, "unliterary" words, primarily to indicate action: *tishkom* (lit. "on the quiet"), *prokralsya* (lit. sneaked, stole). In Batyushkov's time, such words would have been considered better suited to the fable than to the elegy. In any event, neither Dmitriev nor Kapnist would have used them in an elegy or a love poem, whereas in Krylov's fable *The Sack* we find the expression *tishkom* in the conclusion, where he writes of the foolish vanity of the *nouveaux riches*, always in danger of suffering the fate of the fabled

Sack (i.e., of being thrown out as unserviceable should they suffer a sudden reverse of fortune). It may be assumed that Batyushkov had read the fable and may well have followed Krylov's example in using the same word, albeit in a different context.

When the spirit moves him, Batyushkov extends the exposition of his original and introduces new, dynamic details. Parny describes the parting of the lovers at dawn as follows:

> *L'Aurore vint plutôt qu'à l'ordinaire*
> *De nos baisers interrompre le cours;*
> *Elle chassa les timides Amours:*
> *Mais ton souris, peut-être involontaire,*
> *Leur accorda le rendez-vous du soir.*[49]

For this elegant but periphrastic account, Batyushkov substitutes a description of the physical state of the beloved:

> *Rano utrennie rozy*
> *Zapylali v nebesakh . . .*
> *No lyubvi bestsenny slëzy*
> *No ulybka na ustakh,*
> *Tomno persey volnovan'e*
> *Pod prozrachnym polotnom—*
> *Molcha novoe svidan'e*
> *Obeshchali vecherkom.*[50]

> Early bloomed the rose of morning
> Flaming in the skies above . . .
> But the smile on your lips dawning,
> But the priceless tears of love,
> Languorous, your breasts' soft stirring
> 'Neath the flimsy lawn so light—
> Wordlessly combined, conferring
> Another rendezvous—tonight.

The poet does not tell us what he thinks his beloved is feeling, her emotions are conveyed through their outward and physical expression. The poetry recreates the outward expression of the character's inward state. The author does not address the reader directly, does not explain, but shows, thereby giving the reader the opportunity to assess for himself the strength of his heroine's feeling.

Here, as in the opening lines of the poem, Batyushkov continues boldly to introduce "non-elegiac" words. Where Parny writes of the hope of another rendezvous *du soir*, Batyushkov uses the colloquial diminutive *vecherkom* instead of the more dignified *vecherom* which, in fact, would have been closer in spirit to the original.

Still more fundamental are the changes Batyushkov has wrought in the concluding lines of the verse in which the lover expresses his fantastic desire that the gods should shorten the day as much as possible and prolong the night. While Parny expresses the desire by a complex, abstract, and periphrastic proposition, Batyushkov again deliberately simplifies his slightly pompous periods and gives us a homey version of the same desires:

> Should Zeus's right-hand give me power
> Over day and over night:—
> Late the Dawn should sound the hour
> Which puts the shadowed dark to flight!
> Late the Sun should forth come striding
> From his Eastern porch to gaze:
> Gleam out briefly, then go hide him,
> Sink red-faced behind the trees;
> Long the night would lie, deploying
> Shadows cool o'er fields and streams,
> Long would mortals rest, enjoying
> Amorous luxury in dreams.[51]

"The Eastern Porch" of Batyushkov's sun puts this part of the verse into quite a different stylistic key from the original. This "Eastern porch" does not only simplify the wording of the poem and make it more intimate, but introduces an element of fairy tale imagery. In Russian fairy tales it is quite usual for the Sun to stroll out onto the porch of his own home. The appearance of this image in Batyushkov's poem shows the tendency, between 1809 and 1810, to seek a new language for his love lyrics that would express the individual character of his own feelings.

In his translation from Parny's poem *Le revenant*, which he entitled *Prividenie* (*The Spirit*), Batyushkov reworks the text in the same direction. Instead of the flame of "torches," Batyushkov has flames gleaming in a fireplace; where Parny speaks in general terms of his beloved's tresses, Batyushkov specifies that they are chestnut colored.

Batyushkov replaces the tone of elegant badinage by a different attitude to inevitable death; his verse is permeated by the somewhat conventional but nevertheless truly antique, classic, calm expectation of a man who has come to terms with the will of the gods.

Batyushkov's free translation allows him a more logical foundation for showing the power of man's earthly feelings, the power of love even beyond death. It is a definite landmark both on Batyushkov's road to the establishment of his own poetic individuality and in the development of Russian poetry at this time. In 1808, Zhukovsky had published his ballad *Lyudmila,* which revealed to Russian poetry an entirely new world of poetic concepts. A dead bridegroom who bears off his bride to the graveyard as a punishment for her refusal to accept the will of the Creator provides the story line for this ballad of Zhukovsky's, a translation, or rather an adaptation, of Bürger's *Lenore.*

In Batyushkov's poem the lover, reconciled to his death, promises to visit his beloved, but not to frighten her.

Taken as a whole, Batyushkov's poem looks like a clear case of polemics with Zhukovsky's ballad, in which humility and resignation are shown as essential laws of human existence and the loss, the death of the beloved on earth is recompensed beyond the grave.

In his translation of Parny, Batyushkov is in the present world of natural, human sensuality and pleasure in the delights of life. For this reason his "ghost" is not in the very least frightening; it cannot be so, for the simple reason that it has no intention of showing itself to its beloved in any shape or form. The ghost of Parny-Batyushkov desires that only pleasant manifestations betray his presence:

> Should the lily press her petals
> To caress your rising breast,
> Should the fire beneath the mantel
> Flame up bright at your behest,
> Should another flame more secret
> Cause your lovely cheeks to burn,
> Should the belt that I held sacred
> Come unclasped and slither down,—
> Smile to yourself then, my beloved,
> It is I![52]

Working on this dynamic system of showing the outward condition of the characters in his verse as a way of expressing their inner world, their sentiments, Batyushkov did not limit himself to adapting and reworking Parny's verses about the joys of erotic love.

CHAPTER 4

# My Penates

## I *Literary Images*

**D**URING the years 1810 to 1811 Batyushkov divided his life
between Moscow and his property in the village of Khantonova.
At this time he became more closely connected with a new literary
circle, including the young followers of Karamzin—Zhukovsky and
Vyazemsky. In his letters to Gnedich, who was not overly enthusiastic
about his friend's new connections, Batyushkov wrote: "Zhukovsky
is truly gifted, amiable and courteous, and kind. He carries his heart
on his sleeve. . . . I see him often and always with renewed pleasure."[1] Batyushkov was later to remember convivial evenings with
Vyazemsky in one of his best verse letters *To a Friend* (*K drugu,*
1816).

His new friends were delighted with *A Vision on the Shores of the
Lethe* and encouraged Batyushkov to continue the struggle against
the Shishkovites,[2] while he, for his part, found in them like-
minded literary allies and just the kind of moral support which his
youth and comparative inexperience needed. Towards the end of
1811 or the beginning of 1812, Batyushkov wrote a verse letter to
Zhukovsky and Vyazemsky, *My Penates* which won him even
greater literary acclaim than *A Vision on the Shores of the Lethe.*
The popularity of the *Vision* had been to some extent a *succès
de scandale; My Penates* brought the author lasting renown and
immediately placed him among the finest Russian poets of his
generation. Contemporary readers of *My Penates* could not but
notice a certain superficial resemblance between this letter and the
type of epistolary verse current in French eighteenth-century poetry,
in which it was customary for the poet to combine an idealized
picture of his own daily life with a list of his literary antecedents.
Such "letters" were basically a form of literary polemics. Vyazemsky,
when he received Batyushkov's *My Penates,* pointed out the resemblance between the Russian poem and Jean-Baptiste Louis Gresset's
*La Chartreuse* (1747).

The French poet built his very leisurely poem (it contains twice as many verses as Batyushkov's) around one basic idea: the glorification of a life of rustic retirement which is constantly contrasted with the vain literary bustle of the capital, Paris. Gresset's poem is polemical in tone and contains pamphleteering sketches of the poet's literary opponents. Batyushkov's *My Penates* is quite innocent of direct literary polemic. His literary tastes and sympathies are given positive expression in the form of a list of Russian poets whom he considers as models and in the address to his friends, Zhukovsky and Vyazemsky. Of course, Batyushkov's list is polemical in itself, even provocatively so, both with regard to Shishkov and his group, and to the school of Karamzin and Dmitriev but, there are no literary polemics as such in *My Penates*. In the list of favorite authors there is a marked difference of principle between Gresset and Batyushkov. The French poet included in his list not only French, but Greek, Latin, English, and Italian poets, accompanying each one's name with a poetic portrait.

Gresset wrote his poem, at a time when the literature of the early eighteenth century was still a live phenomenon and not a half-forgotten classic. Batyushkov, however, neither could nor would repeat Gresset's list; he needed a peg on which to hang his own literary sympathies and opinions, and this he did quite openly, not hesitating to include his own friends, the young poets Vyazemsky and Zhukovsky in his list of generally acknowledged authors.

In doing this, Batyushkov showed indisputable literary originality since, as Boris Tomashevsky very justly comments: "Such lists had never included young contemporaries, who were relegated to individual letters, but not to general lists of favorite authors."[3]

Let us look back: in his *Vision on the Shores of the Lethe,* the only contemporary Batyushkov had introduced was Krylov. In *My Penates,* on a par with Lomonosov, Derzhavin, and Bogdanovich, all generally acknowledged poets, Karamzin and Dmitriev were portrayed fully and with partisan admiration, and, together with them, Batyushkov's friends Vyazemsky and Zhukovsky. Some of these poetic portraits were the result of long thought and careful polish. For example, the lines on Karamzin originally read:

> His quill a plume from Lel's bright wing,
> His mentor Marmontel,

> Here Karamzin sits writing
> Tales the Muses tell
> Of love and tender feeling
> In cottages or courts,
> Sweet mysteries revealing
> To sentimental hearts.
> Inspired by sentiments
> He gilds the ginger-bread
> Of prose with eloquence,
> And weaves his story's thread
> In smoothest style to wed
> The sweetness of Xenophon
> To all the strength of Robertson. . . .[4]

In this portrait, the narrative art and Sentimentalism of Karamzin, which in fact Batyushkov did not really admire, are emphasized. In the final text, a quite different portrait was substituted:

> For long the son most favored
> Of fantasy sublime,
> Now Karamzin enslaves us
> With tales of olden time,
> How Agathon invites us
> With Plato home to dine . . .
> Now with sweet tales delights us
> Now pictures pleasure's shrine,
> Now tells of Rus' in ancient days
> How, at her history's dawn,
> Here, in the cradle of the brave,
> The Slavic race was born![5]

This new portrait shows us Karamzin the poet, historian, and thinker.

A special place in Batyushkov's poem is occupied by the portrayals of the poets to whom it is addressed: Zhukovsky and Vyazemsky. They are shown through their work. Zhukovsky is portrayed as the poet of heavenly love—of Petrarchian[6] love, as Batyushkov called it:

> Put aside your sorrow
> Zhukovsky, my good friend!
> For time flies like an arrow,

> And flighty joys soon end!
> Let friendship wipe away your tears
> And soothe your melancholy
> And the pale rose of yesteryears
> Blush bright at Cupid's folly.[7]

Vyazemsky is shown in *My Penates* as a fellow-spirit of the author's, a poet of merriment and love:

> True nursling of the Muses
> Oh happy Hedonist!
> You love the clink of glasses
> And songs of tenderness!
> And as the day advances
> And champagne bubbles fizz,
> You love the languorous glances
> Of fair enchantresses.
> And all fame's weary ornament,
> The vanity, the show
> For but one moment's merriment
> You'll give up with a bow![8]

These literary portraits of Batyushkov's friends lent a certain literary reality to the the author himself so that, in depicting his contemporaries, he also portrayed himself. That is, the image Batyushkov created of the author-poet grew into a self-portrait in the context of the authentic portraits of his friends.

## II  *The Literary Image of the Poet*

The literary images of Batyushkov's poet friends in *My Penates* lent the poem a certain documentary value. Though Zhukovsky was already comparatively well-known, for the Russian ballad *Svetlana* had brought him fame, Vyazemsky was a complete beginner, very little known. What struck the Russian readers of *My Penates* was the creation of a self-image of Batyushkov. Derzhavin, Zhukovsky, and Davydov had all worked on the same theme. The originality of *My Penates*, therefore, lay in the way in which the image of the poet was presented, not in the portrayal itself.

Everyone who wrote about Batyushkov in verse after *My Penates* repeated his literary self-portrait by rephrasing his lines and images:

Vyazemsky (1812):

> *Stikhov svoikh igrivykh*
> *Mne svitok prigotov',*
> *Stikhov krasnorechivykh,*
> *Gde druzhbu i lyubov'*
> *Ty serdtsem vdokhnovennoy*
> *Pevets veseliya i bedstviy zhizni nashey*[12]
> .........................................

> A scroll I pray you fashion
> Of your own playful verse
> Wherein of friendship, passion,
> You hold sweet-tongued discourse,
> With unconstrainéd art
> Inspired, straight from the heart.

Zhukovsky (May 1812):

> *Prochti zh, poet bestsennoy,*
> *Puskay zhivut s toboy*
> *V obiteli smirennoy*
> *Posredstvennost', pokoy,*
> *I muza, i kharity,*
> *I lary domovity;*[10]
> .....................

> Read this, dear poet-friend,
> And in your humble dwelling
> The golden mean on you attend
> And peace that passes telling,
> The Muse, and all Three Graces,
> The Lares' homelike faces;
> Be faithful to these spirits,
> Your lyre treat as a game,
> And pay but casual visits
> To the stately halls of Fame.

Pushkin (1814):

> *Filosof rezvy i piit,*
> *Parnassky schastlivy lyubimets,*
> *Napersnik milykh anoid!*
> *Pochto na arfe zlatostrunnoy*
> *Umolknul radostny pevets?*[11]
> Sportive philosopher and bard,
> Sweet Aonides confident,

> Parnassus' favorite, fortune-starred,
> Why are your golden harp-strings still,
> Singer of joy and merriment?

Voeykov (1819):

> *I ty v ventse iz roz, i s pradedovskoy chashey,*
> *Pevets veseliya i bedstviy zhizni nashey*[12]
> . . . . . . . . . . . . . . . . . . . . . . . . . . . . . . .
> And you, rose-crowned, bearing an ancient chalice,
> Fair poet of our lives' delights and malice,
> Luxurious Batyushkov!—Your entrancing power
> Conjures love, wine and song, Fame's fevered hour.
> Horace the Muses' love, sweet-tongued Ovidius Naso,
> Anacreon and you, you honor yet the Graces.

Thus, Batyushkov became identified in the literary consciousness of his time—in the imagination of his literary allies and enemies alike—with the image of the poet he himself had created.

In *My Penates* he put forth a whole program of life based on a proclamation of the poet's complete independence from "the fetters of the court," and the world of self-interest and sycophancy. This program was to be totally devoted to the creation in poetry of a harmonious image of the fullness of life, embodied in the image of the poet, and was to take the place of the real personality of the man—Konstantin Batyushkov.

The image of the poet created by his own verses and in the verses of others addressed to him was accepted as a strictly literary persona—as an ideal, a norm—and not as the reflection of biographically authentic material. An impassable boundary was assumed to lie between life and poetry. Poets write verses about themselves, about poets, and poetry in relation to the world, to history, to humanity, but whatever the scale by which the problem was to be measured, the point of departure was always the living nucleus of poetry—the poet himself, regardless of how slight or deep was the image of his own individual fate. Poets had not yet obtained the right to a biography in poetry, but they were in the process of obtaining the right to a destiny. Zhukovsky became the singer of his own unrequited love; Denis Davydov—a quintessential Hussar officer; Batyushkov—the poet of joyous delight in life. It was impossible for the poet to escape the constraint of his literary destiny. Zhukovsky was forever to remain the singer of sadness, melancholy, separation, hopelessness, whatever he may have written later in life; Davydov, a serious war writer and theoretician of partisan warfare, was doomed to remain, in poetry, the singer "of rum and arrack"; whereas Batyushkov is still to this day considered as the poet of elegant sybaritism although his fate and work were full of genuine, absolutely nonliterary tragedy.

The poem *My Penates* was not without precedent in Batyushkov's work. In 1810 he had reworked *Dreams* (1802) into which he had introduced a completely new image of Horace; instead of the dreamer of Batyushkov's first version there now emerged a poet of love and joy, much like the hero of *My Penates:*

> At lovely Glycera's bashful feet
> You sang, a youthful lover,
> Of love's first victory,
> The blood's first heady fever,
> The heart's first amorous sigh,
> Of Cythera's lusty games
> You sang with heart at ease,
> And all the cares of Fame
> You scattered on the breeze.[13]

There is a great deal of repetition of popular themes in *My Penates*, as well as images in vogue among the poets of Russian Sentimentalism: Muraviev, Karamzin, Dmitriev. The poet, who prefers a life of love and poverty to the Philistine existence of the rich and famous, is one of their favorite motifs.

Usually, this lauding of the poet's poverty is accompanied by a description of his humble pastoral abode in the bosom of Nature, which is contrasted to the magnificent city mansions of the wealthy. By the time Batyushkov began writing *My Penates* all this was the common stock-in-trade of Sentimental poetry, perhaps even already something of an empty convention. So Karamzin, in his poem *To a Poor Poet* (1796), had announced that

> Nature takes a mothers' care
> Of those who in a World unfair
> At birth by Fortune are forsaken
> She gives them wit and warmth of heart,

> And—wondrous gift—the singer's art
> From golden strings fire to awaken
> And hearts with harmony to snare.[14]

And further, as though giving a blueprint for the contents of *My Penates:*

> Send out your jocund verse inviting
> The happy friends you most delight in
> To join you in a plenteous feast . . .[15]

Batyushkov, while following the thematic tradition in the poetry of Russian Sentimentalism, shuffled the component parts, remade them in his own fashion and, most importantly, instead of developing set lyrical themes,[16] created an image of a specific lyrical hero: the image of the poet.

This image in *My Penates* was calculated to be accepted regardless of genre, but the genre of the "friendly letter" made it possible for Batyushkov to create the impression of a poetic personality and to introduce a literary image as a portrait of the author himself.

### III  *Contrasts in Style*

*My Penates* contains no direct polemics with the author's opponents either in literature or society. The whole content of this epistolary poem, its themes, characters, and style, gives artistic expression to his literary opinions. In comparison with the verses of 1809–1810, a new and vital element had appeared in the style of *My Penates,* an element which before that time appears to have arisen in Batyushkov's work more or less fortuitously.

In his struggle against Church Slavonicisms, Batyushkov began to parody the religious and ecclesiastical terminology so much loved by Shishkov, Shikhmatov, and others like them. An example is the poem *To Masha* (1810):

> *O raduysya, moy drug, prelestnaya Maria.*
> *Ty prelestey polna, lyubovi i uma.*
> *S toboyu gratsii, ty gratsiya sama.*
> *Pust' parki vvek pryadut tebe chasy zlatye!*
> *Amur tebya blagoslovil,*
> *A ya—kak angel govoril.*[17]

> Hail and rejoice, my friend, enrapturing Maria,
> Be full of raptures, wisdom, love and health,
> Be full of Grace, for thou art grace itself.
> May Parcae spin for thee a golden Epopeia!
> Cupid has blessed thee—I as well
> Salute thee, like the angel Gabriel.*

As D. D. Blagoy pointed out, the poem parodies the salutation of the Archangel Gabriel: "This poem is a parody of the words addressed by Archangel Gabriel to the Virgin Mary. . . . The first line of Batyushkov's poem is repeated almost word for word by Pushkin in his *Gavriliada:* "Hail and rejoice, Immaculate Maria!"

A similar ironic intermixture of Greek mythology with concepts and names taken from the New Testament is contained in Batyushkov's verse letter to Vyazemsky in reply to his friend's enthusiastic praise of the *Vision on the Shores of the Lethe*:

> *Ty moyu sonlivu "Letu"*
> *V Iordan preobratil*
> *I, smeyasya, mne poetu*
> *Tak* kadilom nakadil . . .[18]

> My sleepy "Lethe" you have sent
> Flowing between the Jordan's banks,
> And laughing, with a censor so incensed
> The poet and his idle pranks. . .

The expression "Kadilom nakadit"—indicating the action of incensing the congregation from a censor swung by the officiating priests or his assistants, repeated at frequent intervals throughout the Orthodox service and thus of everyday use among pious church-goers—is given an ironical twist in this jesting verse, and the River Lethe is transformed into the Jordan. Thus, a very familiar set of proper names and phrases were transferred into a different system of relationships and acquired metaphorical significance, becoming poetic symbols.[19] At the same time, the jest itself, acquires a different meaning; the poet is playing on the collision of

---

*The last line, translated literally, can read either "And I—spoke like an angel," or "And I—like the Angel Gabriel," the second reading being oral, not textual. The pun is a play between *"goveril"—spoke* and *"Gavriil"—Gabriel.*

concepts of various origins and stylistic types. For example, his cupid can *confer a blessing* and he himself can speak *like an angel*. A certain stylistic equality is thereby introduced between concepts of various natures; in Batyushkov's poems these concepts are subjected to the overall tone, the overall mood—in this case, one of easy banter.

Batyushkov also had inconsistencies or incompatibilities in *My Penates*. Thus, for instance, he has an obvious contradiction between what he has to say of each of his poet friends individually and the collective description which precedes the individual portraits. At one point, he calls Zhukovsky and Vyazemsky "carefree favorites of Fortune" ("bespechnye schastlivtsy"), but a few lines further he says that Zhukovsky's life passes under the sign of "tears" and "bitterness" not of freedom from care nor yet of good Fortune. Such contradictions in *My Penates* are neither exceptional nor accidental. The entire poem is composed of poetic formulae combined in a manner that was then rather unusual. Moreover, even within these poetic formulae, it is not difficult to detect combinations of concepts which, within the context, at first sight appear to be mutually exclusive.

Students of Batyushkov's poetry are usually curious about the interesting notes and remarks made by Alexander Pushkin on the margins of Batyushkov's collection *Essays in Prose and Verse*. As has been established by B. L. Komarovich,[20] the majority of these notes were made by Pushkin around 1830, and reflected Pushkin's attitude to Batyushkov's poetic works at a time when the younger poet's literary opinions and talents had attained full maturity after his Southern poems, *Boris Godunov, Poltava, The Little Tragedies*, and *Evgeny Onegin*.

However interesting and instructive Pushkin's notes may be, they cannot yet be considered as absolute criteria for artistic merit.

Pushkin points out the defects of *My Penates,* but at the same time expresses approval in somewhat abstract terms for the poem as a whole, to which he applies the epithet "charming" (*prelestnoe*).

The chief imperfection of the poem is, in Pushkin's view,

the too obvious mixture of the antique customs of mythology with traditions of the inhabitants of the villages around Moscow. The Muses are ideal beings. Our Christian imagination has become accustomed to them, but the "lairs" and "cells" into which the Lares are put transport us too drastically to the interior of the Grecian hut, where we are not at all pleased to encounter a table with torn cloth and, ensconced before the fire, one of Suvorov's soldiers with a two-stringed balalaika. All this is just too contradictory.[21]

Pushkin compares the following lines from the description of the poet's dwelling in *My Penates:*

> Penates of my fathers
> And keepers of my home
> You have no gold or treasures
> And yet you love your own
> Dark cells and lairs, where
> I placed you with so much care,
> Corners here and there adorning
> For the day of my house-warming.
> . . . . . . . . . . . . . . . . . . .
> And before the window
> Of this my humble cot
> Stands a three-legged, spindly
> Table with tattered top.
> . . . . . . . . . . . . . . . . . . .
> But you, my poor blind beggar
> Who limps along the road
> A prey to wind and weather
> Come, knock at my abode,
> And lay your humble crutch aside,
> You're welcome to my home
> To sit till you are warm and dried
> Before the glowing flame.
> Old soldier, grizzled by the rime
> Of labor and of years,
> Wounded by bayonet three times
> In patriotic wars,
> Your two-stringed balalaika
> Will strum up old campaigns . . . [22]

What had seemed to Pushkin, in the 1830's, to be a defect in the artistry of these verses and what because of Pushkin's own achievements had come to be expected as a *sine qua non* of Russian poetry—unity of style in the reproduction of every aspect of the national-cultural tenor of life[23]—had not even been recognized as a problem at the end of the 1810's and beginning of the 1820's. Batyushkov, in his translations of Parny's Scandinavian[24] and Madagascan verses, had sought various poetic means to convey what he considered to be the spirit of Northern or Southern poetry. Nevertheless, he considered his fundamental task as a poet to be the creation of a homogeneous, general, poetic language (*slog*) or style capable of expressing the complexity of the mind of contemporary man. This was what he so appreciated in Ariosto and Tasso, and this was the reason for his search for ways of uniting and forging a single whole from words and concepts which, in the practice of Russian poetry, had hitherto existed separately. He sought to unite extreme, opposing spheres of poetic usage: for example, antique mythological imagery with the terminology of Russian religious odes and metrical psalms, based on the imagery of the Slavonic Bible, particularly of the Psalter.

Batyushkov considered it his task to synthesize these poetic and linguistic spheres notwithstanding the variety of their provenance and, therefore, deliberately risked those mixtures which, twenty years later, were to appear to Pushkin as a defect in his artistry.

The opening lines of *My Penates* are: *Otecheski penaty/ O pestuny moi!*[25]

*Penaty* (Penates) and *pestuny* (keepers, guardians, fosterers) are words taken from completely different spheres of life and literature; the mythological and literary Penates and the homely, somewhat familiar *pestuny* are used by Batyushkov as poetic synonyms for the same concept, thus removing that concept from the sphere of strictly poetical language. However, as both are employed in a figurative sense, they are put on an equal footing.

Throughout the poem Batyushkov repeatedly uses two terms to describe the same object: *No lyubite svoi/Nory i temny kel'i.*[26]

*Kel'i* (cells) and *nory* (lairs) again double one another's meaning, as the poetic term for those places which the poet allots to his domestic gods. In this case, too, one of these concepts—*nory*—is an everyday, household word, whereas the other—*kel'i* is taken from a loftier stylistic stratum and applied in a lowered, figurative sense.

Batyushkov does not imagine his "Penates" as Greek gods of the hearth with their own clearly defined religious and domestic functions, but as the patron-gods of poetry, symbolic of that world of beauty which the poet—that is, Batyushkov himself—inhabits.

Their "cells" and "lairs" are not the hovels of some Greek villager, but poetic designations of that sphere of the spirit in which the poet is most at home.

The confusion between the customs of the inhabitants of the area around Moscow and those of Greek mythology, condemned by Pushkin, are also exaggerated. Why was it assumed that in *My Penates* the countryside depicted is that "around Moscow," and, indeed, what indications are there that the poem has a country setting at all? The poet's "dwelling" as described in *My Penates,* is called something different every time he mentions it:

> Oh, Lares settle down
> In my *retired abode.*
> . . . . . . . . . . . . . .
> In this poor *hovel* here
> . . . . . . . . . . . . . .
> With you in poverty
> This simple *shack* is dear
> . . . . . . . . . . . . . .
> You, Lares and Penates,
> Of this my humble *hut!*
> . . . . . . . . . . . . . .
> Come in a carefree hour,
> Come to my *little house* . . .[27]

It is a sufficiently varied set of appellations for the "quiet corner" inhabited by the poet: *obitel'* (a *retired abode*; the word can mean *cloister*), *khizhina* (a *hovel*), *shalash* (a *shack*), *khata* (a *hut*), *domik* (a *little house*). Not one of these designations or poetic synonyms really serves to describe any real house where the poet might actually live. The following lines, too, run contrary to Pushkin's attempt to localize the poet's abode:

> What matters it if in an unknown land
> In the shadow of dense forests
> By the blind Goddess I was forgotten,
> Still wrapped in swaddling bands . . .[28]

In *Dream* (1802), Batyushkov had already shown that he distinguished perfectly clearly between the poetry of the North

(Ossian) and of the South (Horace). Why then at the moment he attained full poetic maturity, did he permit such obvious and deliberate mixture of widely varying stylistic strata? Where, when all is said and done, does the poet live? Surely the poem itself gives us the answer to this question:

> Not gold nor rank are needed
> As passport to the grace
> Of holy poetry
> And in this peaceful place
> She often visits me.
> When inspiration falls
> Asleep . . . the lucid mind,
> Released from earthly ties,
> Soars through the higher sphere
> And to Aonia flies
> To join the Muses' choir![29]

The poet lives in his own country—the country of poetry—where for companions he has peace, living beauty, love, other poets, the living and the dead, teachers and friends. The world of poetic dream, which, in his early verses—as in the verses of Karamzin and Zhukovsky—existed only as an ideal world totally unconnected with the world of everyday human existence, is depicted as the poet's real life in *My Penates.* And the table with the torn cloth and Suvorov's (?!) soldier with his "two stringed balalaika," just as Lileta in her "military garb," were intended to lend authenticity to this poetic hermit's existence, so as to prevent it from dissolving into the purely literary circumstances of a poetic life.

### IV  *Movement in Verse*

In *My Penates* Batyushkov achieved not only lucidity, precision, and fluency, but what he considered the most important quality of the contemporary poetic manner—"movement." In this connection, raving over a satirical poem by Vasily Pushkin, uncle of the great poet, obviously written under the influence of his own *Vision on the Shores of the Lethe,* Batyushkov wrote to Gnedich on May 29, 1811: "What verses! What pace! What *movement!* And that was written by the languid Muse of Vasily Lvovich!"[30]

By the word "movement" Batyushkov at that time apparently meant a swift succession of subjects in a verse or long poem, the absence of tedious passages, *longueurs,* repetitions, and so on. In *My Penates* Batyushkov achieved increasing movement in this sense; the poem consists of a swift succession of episodes, never pausing, never slowing down over one single line—the invocation of the Penates, the appearance of Lileta, the list of favorite poets, the direct address to his friends, or thoughts of death overcome by the joys of love and creative work.

Batyushkov achieves this movement and pace of poetic language by changes of verb tense, keeping the action moving from present to past or future. In this regard, he also began to criticize the verses of his friends. Thus, Vyazemsky's epistolary poem *To my Mistress* (*K podruge,* 1815), a frank imitation of *My Penates,* was torn to pieces by Batyushkov in a letter to the author.

Batyushkov considered that the opening of some eighteen lines should be compressed, and he wrote to Vyazemsky: "I found the beginning of your letter dragged. This can be easily remedied, all you have to do is to compress everything . . . and not spin out your thoughts into lengthy poetic periods, which repulse the reader and fatigue curiosity. Make the beginning shorter, as short as possible."[31]

But Batyushkov also praised the details of Vyazemsky's poem, especially the antithesis between the contrasting descriptions of "domestic felicity" and the "bustle of society." This is, of course, the same antithesis around which *My Penates* is constructed, where the description of the poet's "poor hovel" and his way of life is contrasted to the life of the rich and famous which he rejects and censures:

> *Ne vina blagovonny,*
> *Ne tuchny fimian,*
> *Poet prinosit vam,*
> *No slëzy umilen'ya*
> *No sertsa tikhiy zhar*
> *I sladki pesnopen'ya,*
> *Bogin' permesskikh dar!*[32]

> Not wine of heady fragrance
> Not clouds of incense sweet
> Does the bard lay at your feet,
> But a still heart's devotion;

> But tears of piety,
> And—Muses' meet oblation—
> Melodious psalmody!

To the world of riches, material abundance, and financial ease—to the world of things, the poet opposes the world of ideas and feelings. He contrasts the real world with an ideal world where men live by the laws of beauty, love, and happiness.

The theme of wealth, "gold," runs through the poem from its very inception:

> *Otecheski penaty,*
> *O pestuni moi!*
> *Vy zlatom ne bogaty ...*[33]
> Penates of my fathers
> And keepers of my home
> You are not rich with gold ...

Gold is mentioned again at the beginning of that part of the poem which deals with poetry and poets:

> *Bez zlata i chestey*
> *Dostupen dobryi geniy*
> *Poezii svyatoy,*
> *I chasto v mirnoy seni*
> *Beseduyet so mnoy.*[34]
>
> Not gold nor rank are needed
> As passport to the grace
> Of holy poetry,
> And in this peaceful place
> She often visits me.

In *My Penates* Batyushkov established his own scale of values, declaring his right to his own particular system of poetic concepts, his own philosophy of happiness, and finally, his own conception of man.

Already, both in his original poetry and in translations, Batyushkov had found the theme of love leading inevitably to the theme of death. In the poem *Elysium* (*Eliziy*), death is nothing but a transition to another world inhabited by poets who have died.

*Tam, pod ten'yu mirtov zybkoy,*
*Nam lyubov' spletet ventsy*
*I prevetlivoy ulybkoy*
*Vstretyat nezhnye pevtsy.*[35]

In the shadows Love will meet us
Weaving wreaths of myrtle leaves,
Smiling, other shades will greet us,
Bards of tenderness and ease.

Death, as Batyushkov depicted it for those who had understood the purpose of life and had devoted their existence to the delights of love and beauty (poetry), is not perdition, not punishment, not the dissolution of personality, but the natural conclusion of man's existence, free of fear and the timorous clinging to an earthly life. Most probably, this attitude to death explains why Batyushkov elected to translate such a poem as Parny's *Le revenant*. This triumph over death, this ultimate victory of love and beauty (that is, poetry, which includes both beauty and love) is shown in *My Penates*.

When the three gaunt sisters
Have no thread left to spin
And we to our ancestors
Are safely gathered in
Good comrades hear us now!
Heed this last plea of ours!
For why must there be mourning
And wailing of hired choirs?[36]

The poet does not wish any sadness or mourning to ensue upon his death:

*I putnik ugadayet*
*Bez nadpisey zlatykh,*
*Chto prakh tut pochivayet*
*Schastlivtsev molodykh!*[37]

The passer-by will guess
Without gilded epitaphs
That here does lie at rest
The dust of happy youths!

The awareness of the brevity of life and the inevitability of death does not goad the poet into outward activity. He lives in the world of his imagination, a world of love and beauty, which gives him a consciousness of superiority not only in daily dealing with mercenary interests and careerist intrigues, but in death itself, for death has no power to deprive the free man of anything whatsoever. The hero of *My Penates* is free of all the tangles which enmesh those who cannot escape the nets of material dependence.

That "movement" which Batyushkov emphasizes in every poet's verses, including his own, is achieved in *My Penates* not only because of swift, sharp, sudden sequences of episodes, but also because of a similar structural composition within many of the single lines. Of no less significance for the dynamics of the poem as a whole is the way in which these episodes constantly overlap and interweave, creating a striking impression of movement and pace, and eliminating all sluggishness and tendency toward such *longueurs* as those which mar some of Batyushkov's other long poems (for example *Dream* (*Mechta*) in the 1810 version). The unexpected simultaneous introduction of two contrasting themes in *My Penates* is a technique which may be traced through any of the poem's episodes.

The portraits of the poet-friends introduce the simultaneous development of two contrasting themes: intoxication with the delights of life and the presentiment of death. He begins with the theme of the feast of life:

> *O! day zhe ty mne ruku,*
> *Tovarishch v leni moy,*
> *I my . . . potopim skuku*
> *V sey chashe zolotoy!*[38]

> Your hand! Good friend of mine,
> Comrade in idleness,
> And we . . . in golden wine
> Will drown world-weariness!

Then Time sends in the bill, recalling the finite nature of all earthly existence and, it follows, the inevitability of death:

> While close behind us lowers
> Grey Time with hasty tread

> And scythes the meadow flowers
> With unrelenting blade.[39]

In the next eight lines both these themes—heady delight in life and the inevitability of death—are given together:

> Hasten down the broad and level
> Highroad to happiness;
> In pleasure we shall revel
> And we shall outrun Death;
> Let us steal the flowers
> From 'neath the flailing scythe,
> Let idleness prolong the hours
> The fleeting hours of life.[40]

Almost every line in this excerpt contains some unexpected twist, some unforeseen collision of meanings, sometimes even distinguished by the way the verse is set out on the page:

> And we . . . in golden wine
> Will drown world-weariness.[41]

Sometimes the unexpectedness of such combinations—the contrast of meaning—is disguised by a conjunction which lends the combination an illusion of causal relationship, which in fact is simply not there:

> In pleasure we shall revel
> *And* we shall outrun death[42]

A similar impression of an apparent connection in the absence of any real causal relationship is given in *My Penates* by the system of anaphoric beginnings of neighboring or even of distant lines, and by the taking up of certain refrains or echoes at the beginnings and ends of major and minor episodes.

The anaphoric opening is used frequently in *My Penates* as a device for linking lines:

> *Not* wine of heady fragrance
> *Not* clouds of incense sweet
> Does the bard lay at your feet—

> *But* the still heart's devotion;
> *But* tears of piety,
>
> . . . . . . . . . . . . . . . .
>
> Until the morning light
> *Serenely* he can browse,
> *Serenely* he can drowse
> Beside his love in sleep!
>
> . . . . . . . . . . . . . . . .
>
> I drink my Lily's breathing
> Upon her ardent lips
> *Like* scented roses wreathing,
> *Like* nectar from festal cups.[43]
>
> . . . . . . . . . . . . . . . .

Another example of the use of the initial anaphora is when it occurs every other line:

> To *povest'yu prelestnoy*
> *Plenyayet Karamzin,*
> To *mudrogo Platona*
> *Opisyvayet nam.*[44]
>
> Now with a charming story
> Karamzin enchants us;
> *Now* it is Plato the Wise
> Whom he describes for us.

Sometimes such initial repetitions are only effected after three or more lines:

> Ty lyubish' *pesninezhny*
> *I ryumok zvon i stuk!*
> *V chas negi i prokhlady*
> *Na uzhinakh tvoikh*
> Ty lyubish' *tomny vzglyady*
> *Prelestnits zapisnykh*[45]
>
> . . . . . . . . . . . . . . . . .
>
> *You love* the clink of glasses
> And songs of tenderness!
> And as the day advances
> And champagne bubbles fizz
> *You love* the languorous glances
> Of fair enchantresses.
>
> . . . . . . . . . . . . . . . . .

Of equal importance in "movement" is the system of echoes linking line to line, as above, but not necessarily at the beginning of the lines:

> Streloyu *mchitsya vremya*
> *Veselie* streloy!
> Time *flies* like an arrow
> And *flighty* joys soon end!

Too, the end of one episode in the poem may contain an echo which is taken up again in the next verse, the next episode:

> This simple shack is dear,
> *Not gold* endears it to me,
> But that your charms are here.
>
> . . . . . . . . . . . . . . . . .
>
> *Not gold* nor rank are needed
> As passport to the grace
> Of holy poetry . . .[46]

The sequence of episodes throughout the poem begin and end abruptly, without any transitions or explanations. At the same time there are frequent changes of tense in the narrative which set off the different episodes.

The various devices used by Batyuskov in *My Penates* made this poem a model of the new genre, while the image of the poet —himself—in this epistolary poem was one which became a "type" for poets for several years to come.

CHAPTER 5

# The Elegy

### I  *Poetry and War*

IN January 1812, full of literary plans and rather vague hopes of establishing himself in the civil service, Batyushkov returned to Petersburg. Thanks to Alexey Olenin, the director of the Public Library, he was appointed a member of the library staff as Assistant Keeper of Manuscripts, where his old friend Gnedich and Ivan Krylov were his colleagues. During their evening hours of duty, Gnedich's writer friends would drop in, and Batyushkov found them congenial company. At the same time he kept up a lively correspondence with his Moscow friends, Vyazemsky and Zhukovsky. At first, these letters were almost entirely devoted to literary themes, but soon the novelty of the periodical press and the jesting verses gave way to political news and speculation: Napoleon's forces had crossed the Neman and Russia was once more involved in a war with France, a war destined to prove desperately perilous and to bring great hardship.

Batyushkov wished to rejoin his regiment, but was temporarily delayed by sickness. A few days before the Battle of Borodino—after which Moscow was occupied by the French—Batyushkov arrived in Moscow at the request of the widow of his old teacher, Ekaterina Fyodorovna Muravieva, to help her and her children to evacuate to the interior of Russia.

While the fate of Moscow and the outcome of the war was being decided by the battle between the two armies, Batyushkov was in Moscow waiting "in inexplicable terror" to hear about the outcome of the fighting. When Ekaterina Fyodorovna decided to leave for Nizhny Novgorod (now Gorky), Batyushkov accompanied her. There they found a great gathering of Muscovites, and even here aristocratic Moscow retained its usual manners and habits. Batyushkov was disgusted by this society devoid of serious ideas or any sense of its true social obligations: "Wherever you turn there are sighs, tears—and foolishness," he wrote Gnedich. "Everyone complains and blames the French in French, but patriotism is expressed in the phrase: *point de paix*."[1]

Meanwhile Batyushkov's desire to take part in the war was not being fulfilled as quickly as he had hoped. In February 1813 he returned to Petersburg and one month later he joined the Rylsky Infantry Regiment. It was July before he was assigned to the Russian Army at Dresden, where general Nikolay Nikolaevich Raevsky, one of the great heroes of the war, made him his adjutant. At Raevsky's side, Batyushkov served through the liberating campaigns of 1813 and 1814, took part in the Battle of Leipzig, and participated in the siege and taking of Paris, which he describes in one of his letters:

I saw Paris, shrouded in dense fog, an endless row of buildings dominated by Notre Dame with its tall towers. I confess my heart beat fast with joy. . . . All the heights were occupied by artillery, another moment and Paris would be crumbling beneath a rain of shells! Should one wish for this? The French sent out an officer to parley and the cannon fell silent. Wounded Russian officers passed us and congratulated us on the victory: "Glory be to God! We've reached Paris sword in hand." "Moscow is avenged!" The soldiers echoed them, bandaging their wounds.[2]

After the cessation of hostilities, Batyushkov stayed in Paris for two months, and then returned to Petersburg via England, Sweden, and Finland.

From that time on, that is, from the middle of 1814, began the most fruitful period of Batyushkov's poetic work. He wrote much in verse and prose, and began to prepare for publication his collection, *Essays in Verse and Prose,* which came out in October 1817. Batyushkov now felt the strength and maturity of his talent and he also received long overdue recognition from critics and the public.

The War of 1812 and the war during the next years (1813–14) had a profound influence on Batyushkov, forcing him to reexamine fixed, and—as he had thought—firmly rooted convictions. He was shattered by the burning of Moscow and for some time he utterly rejected his attachment to the philosophy of the French Enlightenment, seeing in the French nothing but enemies: "I have too lively a perception of the wounds inflicted upon our beloved country to know one moment's tranquility. The terrible actions of the Vandals—the French—in Moscow and its suburbs, actions without precedent in history, have completely upset my small philosophy and put me out of charity with mankind,"[3] he wrote to Gnedich in October 1812 under the fresh impression of what he had seen. To Vyazemsky he wrote that he now found the whole century of Enlightenment detestable because it had prepared the way for Napoleon: "Moscow is no more! What irredeemable losses! The death of friends, this sacred place, this peaceful sanctuary of learning, all defiled by a horde of barbarians! Here are the fruits of Enlightenment or, it would be truer to say, of the perversion of the cleverest of peoples . . . How much ill has been done! When will there be an end to it? On what can we base our hopes? In what take pleasure? Yet life without hope, without pleasure—is not life, but anguish!"[4]

In the course of the military actions leading to the defeat of Napoleon and to the liberation of the peoples of Europe from French domination, Batyushkov shook off some of the extremes of his Francophobia and tried to understand the historical significance of these "important events."

He now came to the conclusion that every thinking person should review and reevalute his attitude toward the philosophy of the Enlightenment in the light of the historical experience of the last twenty years. Batyushkov set forth his altered views in several articles subsequently included in his *Essays*. Both extremes of his previous attitude to life, Epicureanism and Stoicism, he found wanting, denying that they corresponded to the needs of contemporary man or to the spirit of modern times. The theory of reasonable egoism he criticized for what seemed to him too low an estimate of man's intrinsic worth:

For these philosophers friendship and love, the feeling of a son for his father, the most tender feeling of a mother for her offspring—in a word: gratitude or disinterestedness—and all that mankind possesses that is precious, beautiful, great; all the impulses of generosity, all the involuntary promptings and secret sacrifices of the noble heart; all are products of self-interest.[5]

The philosophy of Stoicism Batyushkov identified with the morality of "the interest of the State" first advanced by the Jacobins and supported by Napoleon, which justified any violence if it were considered expedient by the government: "The Stoic system is fallacious," wrote Batyushkov, "because its morality is based on mere intellectualism, on nothing but denial; it is fallacious because it wages ceaseless war upon the tenderest family attachments which are based on love, on benevolence . . . but to the heart it has nothing to say."[6] Now, Batyushkov doubted even the very same philosophy of happiness and pleasure which he had himself so eagerly expressed in his verses of 1809–1811, particularly in *My Penates*. "The multitudinous troop of Epicurean philosophers from Montaigne to the stormiest days of revolution kept telling man: Rejoice! The whole of nature is yours, it offers you its sweets, all the intoxications of mind, heart, imagination, and feelings; everything, except hope in the future, everything is yours, momentary but certain!"[7]

Doubt in all philosophical systems, the thought of the relative and limited quality of each and every one of them, forced Batyushkov to the conclusion that "mortals require a *morality* founded on divine revelation, for this alone can serve at all times and in all circumstances; it is the shield and spear of the good man which times does not rust."[8]

From this, however, one should not conclude that Batyushkov turned to religion, experienced a crisis in his beliefs, or even, as he himself wrote, suffered the collapse of his "small philosophy."

What had happened was something different—a very significant broadening of Batyushkov's life experience, both practical and spiritual, which he was seeking to rationalize in the light of the historical events he had witnessed and participated in: "To undertake even the most limited social activity, it is very necessary to have a conviction of certain constant moral truths to support one's own weakness."[9]

Batyushkov was unable to establish any connection or any satisfactorily motivated similarity whatsoever between individual human existence which could and would subject itself to moral laws and the development of historical events. Between these two he saw only an impassable abyss.

Religion now seemed more convincing to him. He saw in it a more substantial filling for that emptiness of soul which he felt in himself and in men of his generation, an emptiness left by unfilled hopes born of the victorious wars fought between 1812 and 1815. These hopes were swiftly shattered by the reactionary politics implemented by the Holy Alliance throughout Europe and, of course, Russia.

The complex mutual interaction of political events and changes, and the poet's personal experience appreciably broadened the range of his creative thought. Batyushkov transformed the elegy. This genre, hitherto confined to the description of certain definite sentimental situations, began to convey a broader spectrum of the thoughts and emotions of the poet, who sees himself as representative of the spirit of his time—as a man of his epoch. Batyushkov's elegy was already something different from the genre of predetermined theme and style recognized by the literary theoreticians of eighteenth-century Classicism. It had room for a variety of themes and motifs and had become a synthesis embodying all that which ten years later—in the poetry of Pushkin—become known simply as lyric poetry without any specific differentiation of genres.

Batyushkov impregnates the elegy with themes that before him had been held proper only to the ode or to the long poem. One of the new subjects for elegiac poetry was war: motifs of war, memories of war and, finally, entire elegies devoted to incidents of war perceived through the prism of the poet's biography, or told by him in the first person as by an eyewitness, as his own recollections. The themes of war and scenes of war, according to a tradition originated by Lomonosov and continued by all the outstanding poets of the eighteenth century, had been confined to the genre of the solemn ode. Karamzin, Dmitriev, and their followers had eschewed the ode altogether, seeking to avoid the necessity of repeating official dedications and the obligatory laudatory addresses to tsars and highly placed nobles.

By the beginning of the nineteenth century, the ode as a genre had died out and was in use only among the diehards of Classicism.

The wars against France which began in 1805 and ended in 1815, particularly the War of 1812, had given rise to a great wave of patriotism in Russia which found expression in drama and poetry. This was why Zhukovsky and Batyushkov both found inspiration in military and civic themes, but sought new means of expression outside the ode and outside the odic hierarchy of persons and events. They wished to work on the theme of war from a different poetic angle, to introduce the pathos of personal opinion and individual involvement in the common, nationwide struggle. Zhukovsky achieved outstanding success in his treatment of heroic and patriotic themes in his *A Minstrel in the Camp of Russian Warriors* (*Pevets*

*vo stane russkikh voinov*) written toward the end of 1812. Material
and themes which had been common in the ode, Zhukovsky blended
with motifs from the elegy and from the love lyric. In *A Minstrel in
the Camp of Russian Warriors* the tone never alters; with equal
intensity the poet speaks of his love for his motherland and of his
own beloved, praises the heroism of generals and common soldiers,
and recalls the countryside around his home. This approach to war
as an event of personal significance brought Zhukovsky true fame
and linked his name forever with the War of 1812.

Batyushkov, like Zhukovsky, rejected the ode as a genre. Into
his pre-1812 verses, war entered only insofar as it had influenced his
own destiny. War, battle, and a serious wound had been incorporated
into the elegy, *Reminiscences of 1807;* in a lighter vein were certain
anecdotes of military service which appear in Batyushkov's
humorous letters to his friends.

The shocks which the poet experienced in 1812, particularly the
burning and sacking of Moscow, forced him to experience war as a
theme which had organically entered his consciousness. The letter
*To Dashkov,* written in March 1813, was one of the most significant
reactions of Russian poetry to the War of 1812. This work reflects
Batyushkov's impressions of his three visits to Moscow after the
expulsion of the French troops. He wrote to Gnedich:

From Tver to Moscow and from Moscow to Nizhniy, I saw, saw whole
families of all classes, all ages, in the most pitiable circumstances; I saw
what I could not have seen either in Prussia or in Sweden: the transmigra-
tion of entire provinces! I saw want, despair, fires, hunger, all the horrors
of war and, awestruck, I turned my eyes to earth, to heaven, and to myself.[10]

As has been said by one student of Batyushkov's work "these lines
represent a prose conspectus of the beginning of the letter *To
Dashkov,* which gives us an eyewitness picture of the terrible
devastations caused by the Napoleonic invasion."[11]

> *Moy drug! Ya videl more zla*
> *I neba mstitel'nogo kary:*
> *Vragov neistovykh dela,*
> *Voynu i gibel'ny pozhary.*
> *Ya videl sonmy bogachey,*
> *Begushchikh v rubishchah izdrannykh,*

*Ya videl blednykh materev,*
*Iz miloy rodiny izgnannykh!*
*Ya na rasput'e videl ikh,*
*Kak,k persyam chad prizhav grudnykh,*
*Oni v otchayan'e rydali*
*I s novym trepetom vzirali*
*Na nebo rdyanoe krugom.*[12]

My friend! I saw a sea of woes,
Avenging strokes of Heaven's ire:
The furious ragings of our foes
And War, and devastating fire.
I saw the rich pass by in hosts
In tattered garments, fleeing from the wrath,
I saw young mothers, pale as ghosts,
From their dear homeland driven forth!
On open road I saw them where
Their infants to their breasts they clasped,
And standing, sobbing, in despair,
With awestruck eyes looked up, and gasped
To see the whole sky round them red.

This letter gives not only a picture of Moscow's ruins in contrast with her former beauty and splendor, but also the poet's polemical renunciation of the former themes of his work:

*A ty, moy drug, tovarishch moy,*
*Velish' nme pet' lyubov' i radost',*
*Bespechnost', schast'e i pokoy*
*I shumnuyu za chashey mladost'!*
. . . . . . . . . . . . . . . . . .
*Net, net! Poka na pole chesti*
*Za drevniy grad moikh otsov*
*Ne ponesu ya v zhertvu mesti*
*I zhizn',i k rodine lyubov'* . . .
. . . . . . . . . . . . . . . . . .
*Moy drug, dotole budut mne*
*Vse chuzhdy muzy i kharity,*
*Venki, rukoy lyubovi svity,*
*I radost' shumnaya v vine.*[13]

And you, good friend and comrade mine,
You'd have me sing of love and bliss,

> And noisy youth that joys in wine,
> Repose, delight, light-heartedness!
>
> . . . . . . . . . . . . . . . . . . . . . . . . . .
>
> No, no, for until on honor's altar
> I have not laid in sacrifice,
> To avenge the city of my fathers,
> My love of country and my life . . .
>
> . . . . . . . . . . . . . . . . . . . . . . . . .
>
> My friend, till then I do forswear
> The Muses' and Charites' shrine,
> The wreaths Love weaves to bind our hair,
> And all the noisy joys of wine!

Thus, even in rejecting the themes and images of his prewar poetry, Batyushkov reproduces its fundamental motifs in precise detail. All his poetry of pleasure lives on here, only it receives another place; it is temporarily pushed out to the fringe, yielding the center to the poet's heroic and patriotic impulse.

In this poem, Batyushkov remained essentially true to himself. The attitude to war and to the themes of war expressed in the epistolary poem *To Dashkov* was to remain with Batyushkov throughout the rest of his working life. In his elegies, he did not wish to separate the theme of war from other themes which he himself had introduced into the genre, extending its range and the volume of its contents and significance. To blend war with the life of the heart, to show its influence on the mentality and on the personality, and to reveal its psychology was Batyushkov's aim when war became an integral feature of his poetry. In his notebook for 1817 he made the following entry: "Tender thoughts, passionate dreams, and love seem somehow to merge very naturally with the noisy, violent, active life of war."[14]

In almost all his elegies, in every poem written between 1814 and 1817, there was some direct or indirect reflection of war, sometimes as part of a general picture of the trials of the poet's life:

> *Naprasno pokidal stranu moikh otsov,*
> *Druzey dushi, blestyashchie iskusstva,*
> *I v shume groznykh bitv, pod teniyu shatrov*
> *Staralsya usypit' vstrevozhennye chuvstva.*[15]

(*Razluka,* 1815).

> I never should have left my fathers' well-loved land,
> My closest friends, the brilliant realms of art,
> To seek in battle din, 'neath the rough roofs of camp
> Some opiate to sooth my unquiet, restive heart.
>
> (*Separation,* 1815).

At other times, war is the starting point of an everwidening circle of lyrical emotions, for conjuring a whole period of the poet's life tied up—for example—with the life of a friend. Thus, the thought of a fallen comrade revives the memory of a sorrowful episode that took place during the war:

> *Ne ya li nad tvoey bezvremennoy mogiloy,*
> *Pri strashnom zareve Belloninykh ogney,*
> *Ne ya li s vernymi druz'yami*
> *Mechom na dereve tvoy podvig nachertal*
> *I ten'v nebesnuyu otchiznu provozhal*
> *S mol'boy, rydan'em i slezami?*
> *Ten' nezabvennogo! otvetstvuy, milyy brat!*
> *Ili proteksheye vsë bylo son, mechtanye;*
> *Vsë, vsë—i blednyy trup, mogila i obryad,*
> *Svershennyy druzhboy v tvoye vospominan'ye?*[16]

> Was it not I who stood beside your grave untimely
> Lit by the dreadful glow of fierce Bellona's torch,
> Not I, by comrades true befriended,
> Who with the sword carved out the legend of your deed
> Upon a tree and, sobbing, bid your Shade Godspeed
> And to its home divine commended?
> Oh, well-remembered Shade! Come, answer, brother dear!
> Or was all that has passed mere dream, imagination;
> All, all—the pallid corpse, the open grave, the tears,
> The hasty obsequies, friendship's commemoration?

The poet sees in war not only destructive and terrible consequences for mankind; war and the military profession also appear to him as a source of beauty and joy. This is the spirit of the elegy, *The Crossing of the Rhine* (*Perekhod cherez Reyn,* 1817); in a still more major key is the epistolary poem *To Nikita* (*K Nikite,* 1817).

In this poem, war is shown as it might appear in the dreams of a young officer who has not yet had the opportunity of proving his mettle in serious, decisive battles. This point of view explains why

Batyushkov here describes a war of brief engagements and minor battles. Only a very youthful officer could imagine such a cheerful bravura and merry picture of war as the following:

> *Kakoye schast'e, rytsar' moy,*
> *Uzret' s nagornye vershiny*
> *Neobozrimy nashikh stroy*
> *Na yarkoy zeleni doliny!*
> *Kak sladko slyshat' u shatra*
> *Vecherney pushki gul dalekiy*
> *I pogruzit'sya do utra*
> *Pod teploy burkoy v son glubokiy.*[17]

> What happiness, brave knight of mine!
> To look down from some lofty height
> And see our troopers, line on line,
> Ranged on the valley's verdure bright!
> How sweet in camp as evening falls
> To hear the cannon's distant thunder
> And, till the morning bugle calls,
> In your warm Cossack cloak to slumber.

The delight and gaiety running through this poem are achieved not only by the dynamic pace, the swift succession of episodes linked by anaphoric opening words as in *My Penates: Kak* ya lyublu (*How* I love), *Kakoye* schast'ye (*What* happiness), *Kak* sladko (*How* sweet), *Kak* veselo (*What* fun), but also by the choice of adjectives and adverbs:

> Na *yarkoy* zeleni doliny . . .
> On the valley's verdure *bright* . . .
> Kak *sladko* slyshat' . . .
> How sweet to hear. . . .
> I v *vyalom* mire ne nakhodit
> *Otradnoy* serdtsu tishiny.
> And in the *listless* world he finds not
> That stillness which makes *glad* the heart

Such epithets tend to render the emotional and psychological situation of the verse more vivid, based on the paradoxical character of the theme of war and fighting, seen as delight and happiness.

The contrast between war and the joys of life on which the poem *To Dashkov* is based was resolved without sacrificing either theme. In his *Letter to Nikita*, Batyushkov managed to weave the two themes into such an emotional unity that the contrast itself became redundant. In his mature work it was neither the theme nor the genre, but the attitude of the poet as a reflection of his personality which became the definitive criterion for the artistic elaboration of anything life might offer. Batyushkov thought a great deal about picturing contemporary warfare in his poetry: "I would not hesitate to say that . . . modern battles are more picturesque than those of ancient times and therefore more suited to poetry," he wrote in his 1817 Notebook. Reading Tasso, he marked expressions which struck him as particularly suitable to describe Russian soldiers.[18] For the picture of the battle at the beginning of the letter *To Nikita* he made use of the *sirventes* of Guillaume de Saint-Gregory, which he had read in Jean-Charles Leonard de Sismondi's *Littérature du midi de l'Europe,* Paris, 1813.[19]

## II   *Voices from Ages Past*

Interest in war and in themes of war was a manifestation of Batyushkov's interest in history—comparing ancient and modern aspects of European peoples. His endeavor to make sense of the historical experience of humanity found expression in a particular type of elegy, called "historical" by his contemporaries. For Batyushkov, "historical" was synonymous with "national," the expression of a way of thinking and an attitude to life inherent in any nation. In direct contrast to the philosophy of the Enlightenment which sought the common or the similar between different peoples, the forerunners of European Romanticism had begun to take an interest in what was particular and unique in each national culture. For this reason they had begun to look at religion neither as simple error nor as prejudice, but as the legitimate offspring of the spirit of the nation and the form given to a national way of life and thought.

Thus, in *The Crossing of the Rhine,* one of the most important episodes is an Orthodox Church service in which Russian troops take part, preparing themselves to continue the war against Napoleon, and to carry the action onto French territory:

*No tam gotovitsya, po maniyu vozhdey,*
*Beskrovny zhertvennik sred' gibel'nykh trofeev,*
*I bogu sil'nykh Makkaveev*
*Kolenopreklonën sluzhitel' altarey:*
*Ego, shumya, priosenyaet*
*Znamën otchizny grozny les,*
*I solntse yunoe s nebes*
*Altar' siyan'em osypaet.*
*Vse kriki brannye umolkli, i v ryadakh*
*Blagogovenie vnezapu votsarilos',*
*Oruzh'e dolu preklonilos',*
*I vozhd', i ratniki chelo sklonili v prakh:*
Poyut vladyke vyshney sily,
Tebe, podatelyu pobed,
Tebe, nezakhodimy svet!
*Dymyatsya mirnye kadily.*[20]

But there is now prepared at the great men's commands
A bloodless altar set amid grim trophies.
Before the Mighty God of Maccabeus
The priest now kneels in prayer with meekly folded hands.
A rustling forest round him towers,
The colors of the regiments
The young sun from high heaven's tents
The altar with bright glory showers,
All martial shouts have ceased, the ranks are hushed,
A sudden reverence has stilled their warlike bruit:
Their weapons lowered in salute
The leader and the men bow foreheads to the dust
*The most high Lord of Hosts invoking.*
*To Thee, Great God of Victories,*
*To Thee, Oh Light that never dies!*
Pacific mists of incense smoking.

    The phraseology and style of this excerpt deliberately lean toward the vocabulary of the Old and New Testaments. The Old Testament and Apocryphal phrases about the God of the Maccabees and the Lord in the Highest (*i bogu sil'nykh Makkaveev, Poyut vladyke vyshney sily*), the reminiscences of prayers and psalmody (*nezakhodimy svet, Light that never dies*), and the description of the Orthodox ritual itself, were all intended by the author to reproduce the spirit, the mood, and the mental state of the Russian troops on the eve of a great historical occasion. In this particular case, Batyushkov uses the national religion as an inalienable, most characteristic, and most picturesque feature of the culture of his nation.

In another historical elegy *The Dying Tasso* Batyushkov gives in Tasso's monologue a poeticized version of death as it might have appeared to the poet, a devout Catholic and ardent eulogizer of the Crusades:

> *"Smotrite,"—on skazal rydayushchim druz'yam,—*
> *"Kak tsar' svetil na zapade pylaet!*
> *On, on zovët menya k bezoblachnym stranam,*
> *Gde vechnoe svetilo zasiyaet . . .*
> *Uzh angel predo mnoy, vozhaty onykh mest;*
> *On osenil menya lazurnymi krylami . . .*
> *Priblizh'te znak lyubvi, sey táinstvenny krest . . .*
> *Molitesya s nadezhdoy i slezami . . .*
> *Zemnoe gibnet vsë . . . i slava, i venets . . .*
> *Iskusstv i muz tvoren'ya velichavy,*
> *No tam vsë vechnoe, kak vechen sam tvorets,*
> *Podatel' nam ventsa nebrennoy slavy!"*[21]

> "Look to the West,"—so spoke he to his weeping friends—
> "In what a blaze goes down the Primal Light!
> He, he it is who calls me to those cloudless lands,
> Where eternal Day shall break upon our sight . . .
> I see the angel-guide to those bright realms above:
> Cerulean, sheltering wings beat off my fears.
> Put to my lips this cross, emblem of sacred love . . .
> And join your prayers with mine in hope and tears . . .
> All earthly things must fail . . . the laurel crowns and fame . . .
> And Arts' and Muses' splendid story,
> There all eternal is, as God is e'er the same,
> Bestower of the unfading crown of glory."

Further, in explanation of these words, the dying poet speaks of the Catholic faith as the source of his ideas and the foundation of his conception of the world.

Tam vsë velikoe, *chem dukh pitalsya moy,*
Chem ya dyshal ot samoy kolybeli . . .[22]

Therein are all great thoughts *whereon my spirit fed*
The atmosphere I breathed even from the cradle . . .

Of course, there is much open to argument in such an interpretation of Tasso's poetry; in the work of the author of *Jerusalem Delivered* the poetry of great deeds done in the name of religion often yielded place to a glorification of man—the might of his mind and the scale of his endeavors—which accorded completely with the ideas of Renaissance Humanism. Batyushkov, however, was interested in reproducing those specific features which made Tasso the poet of his country and his time. That is why he showed him on his death bed as such a convinced adherent of Catholicism. And, so as to leave his readers in no doubt, Batyushkov, in his notes to *The Dying Tasso,* quotes Tasso's words to one of his friends, words which bear witness to the intense religious aspirations of the poet's last days.[23]

These attempts to reproduce various states of mind and national temperaments show one of the directions in which Batyushkov wished to develop his work. Very revealing for his methods and aims in 1816–17 was his translation-adaptation of Charles-Hubert Millevoye's elegy, *Combat d'Homère et d'Hésiode.* Batyushkov dedicated this translation to Alexey Olenin, but not without hesitation. He left it to Gnedich, who acted as the publisher of the elegy, to decide whether or not to let the dedication stand.[24] Evidently the doubt arose in Batyushkov's mind since he had chosen this elegy for translation because of the correspondence between the ideas and the way in which the subject was set out with certain ideas of his own. These ideas, in some essentials, did not correspond to the literary notions of either Olenin or Gnedich. For all his love of Homer and his admiration for Gnedich's labor as translator of the *Iliad,* Batyushkov differed from his old friends in that he was a convinced supporter of the *petits genres,* that is of the elegy and the epistolary poem, which Gnedich considered mere trifles.

Batyushkov occupied a special position in those discussions on the destiny and principles of art which went on in Olenin's home. In the article *A Stroll Through the Academy of Arts*

(1814), he expressed his views on Russian art most fully. He wrote in the form of a friendly letter, which enabled him to treat his subject in a free, spontaneous manner. Later, when he was preparing to reprint this article in *Essays,* he consulted Gnedich:"We ought to ask Olenin whether we may print it or not. The canvas is his, the silk is mine."[25] Even from this brief remark it is a fair conclusion that *A Stroll Through the Academy of Sciences,* for all the similarity in certain general points of view, contains also a fair admixture of the poet's own opinions, not identical with Olenin's.

The originality of Batyushkov's position lay in his consistent denial of the value of imitating authors of the Ancient World and, at the same time, in his affirmation that modern art had its own particular problems. One of those who accompanies him on his "stroll," a "young artist" somewhat bolder than his companions, does not hesitate to criticize the Ancients. About a plaster copy of a mounted statue of Marcus Aurelius he says: "Modern artists have more skill in the sculpting of horses. We have before our eyes the work of Falconet, this wonderful stallion, alive, fiery, magnificent. And the pose—so bold."[26] Further, a difference arises about Egorov's picture "The Tormenting of Christ." Opinion is divided. The "young artist" praises Egorov's picture, but Starozhilov, another member of the party, disagrees with him: "Unfortunately, the figure is reminiscent of pictures of Christ by other artists and I fail to see the least originality in the picture as a whole, anything new, out of the common, in a word, any original thought, not borrowed from some other source."[27] The author himself takes no part in this argument, but his taste is clearly indicated when he praises the works of a contemporary artist. "With what pleasure, though, we turned to contemplate the portraits of Mr. Kiprensky, the favorite painter of our public. His faultless and exceptionally agreeable drawing, the freshness, harmony and vigor of his colors all combine to demonstrate his talent, the refinement of his mind, and his delicate, cultivated taste."[28]

This evaluation of Kiprensky's pictures tells us a great deal. Russian twentieth-century art historians consider Kiprensky to have been "the true creator of the early nineteenth-century Russian portrait."[29] The critic we have just quoted establishes a direct analogy between the canvases of Kiprensky and the poetry of Batyushkov:

In the friendly correspondence and epistolary poems of Batyushkov, Gnedich, and the early Pushkin we perceive the lineaments of the personages who look out at us from Kiprensky's portraits. These letters are founded on a serene conviction of the existence of general principles which form the basis for the human as well as the natural order. Belief in the possibility of an earthly incarnation of the ideal fills this poetry with youthful high spirits, and a vigorous attachment to the world and its earthly joys. This is the mood to which we owe such masterpieces as Batyushkov's *My Penates* and Pushkin's *Small Town (Gorodok)*![30]

Batyushkov, through the words of his other characters in the *Stroll through the Academy of Arts,* does not merely criticize Egorov for imitating the Ancients and the artists of the Renaissance; he fails to find in his picture anything original.[31] Batyushkov was against mechanical, unreflecting imitation of models and master-pieces of the Ancient World, and in favor of a contemporary art in which the study of the great masters of the past was to be merely a preparatory stage to the creation of new forms corresponding to the content suggested by a New Age. In another article, Batyushkov wrote disapprovingly of an artist who "up till this day has painted nothing original, but only slavishly imitated Raphael, whereas he is quite capable of inventing something of his own, for he has the mind, heart, and imagination."[32] The same vehement negation of the imitative and the affirmation of contemporaneity and, it follows, of creative originality, make themselves felt in the conversation between the critics of Egorov at the Academy of Arts: "The artist wished to paint an academic figure and painted it admirably; but it is not just difficulties overcome that I look for in a picture. I look for more: I look for nourishment for the mind, for the heart; I want it to produce a strong impression on me, to leave a lasting memory in my heart, as a fine play does, if it shows some important, touching matter."[33]

### III  *Batyushkov and Millevoye*

This insistence that a work of art should leave a "lasting memory" and should provide "nourishment for the mind, for the heart" amounts to a general statement of Batyushhkov's aesthetic program. But to return to his differences with Olenin and Gnedich: how were these differences expressed in his article?

It is possible to form a fair estimate of the character and significance of these differences from one of Batyushkov's translations from Millevoye. In a letter to Gnedich, Batyushkov called the elegy *Combat d'Homère et d'Hésiode* "beautiful" and found that "it breathes antiquity."[34]

The subject chosen by Millevoye—a competition between Homer and Hesiod—goes back to early antique sources, to Plutarch, among others. Batyushkov's translation is called simply *Geziod i Omir—Soperniki (Hesiod and Homer—Rivals)*.

Batyushkov considered Millevoye a "real talent" and "one of the best French poets of our time."[35] His translation follows the original closely; even so, the adaptations, corrections, and changes which he does make, essentially alter the stylistic structure of the piece.

Batyushkov has one hundred twenty-six lines to Millevoye's one hundred four, and more variety of rhyme and rhythm. The introduction (twenty-two lines) consists of alternating four-foot and three-foot amphibrachic lines, of which only the three-foot lines rhyme. Millevoye's poem is entirely in alexandrines. The actual announcement inaugurating the competition is written in a complex combination of six-foot and three-foot iambs.

The poet's speeches and the conclusion "from the author" are written in iambic lines of six feet. The rhyme scheme in Hesiod's speeches varies: in his first and third it is *abba*, in the second and fourth *abab*; in the fifth *aabb*.

In all of Homer's speeches the rhyme scheme is *abba*, with the exception of the fifth, which consists of two quatrains with alternating rhymes.

The conclusion from the author is preceded by a quotation, the first and fourth lines of which contain four iambic feet, the second and third—six each.

Thus, the elegy's more complex rhythmic structure and rhyme scheme were in themselves indicative of a serious departure from the original. Batyushkov consistently rid his translation of periphrase, witticisms, and unnatural similes.

Thus, instead of "Nouveaux Automédons" Batyushkov has "voznitsy" (drivers or, presumably in the context, "charioteers").

In Millevoye's original, Hesiod says to Homer:

> *Tu maudiras la vie et le jour où ta mère*
> *Reçut l'embrassement de l'amoureux Mélès*[36]

Batyushkov replaces this polite periphrasis with the direct:

> *. . . ty budesh' proklinat'*
> *I den', kogda na svet tebya rodila mat'.*[37]
>
> . . . and you will come to curse
> The very day on which our mother gave you birth!

In one of Homer's speeches Millevoye puns on the title of Hesiod's *Work and Days:*

> *Des* Travaux et des Jours *tu chantas l'ordonnance;*
> *Pour moi, faible vieillard que le temps a glacé*
> *Les travaux sont finis et les jours ont cessé.*[38]

Batyushkov, while retaining the sense, made no attempt to reproduce the word-play:

> *Ty pel* Trudy i Dni . . .
> *Dlya startsa vetkhogo uzh konchilis' oni*[39]
>
> You sang of *Works and Days* . . .
> They both are over now for my declining age.

Batyushkov made a more precise distinction than did Millevoye between the individual styles of Hesiod and Homer. The style of Batyushkov's Hesiod is—transmuted to the literary scene of 1816— that of "light poetry." Instead of Millevoye's lines characterizing the poetry of Hesiod in the most general terms, Batyushkov speaks of it as though he were another elegist. Where Millevoye writes:

> *Hésiode redit sur un mode plus doux . . .*[40]

Batyushkov has:

> *A yuny Geziod, vzeleyanny Parnasom,*
> *S chudesnoy prelest'yu vospel veselym glasom:*[41]
>
> But youthful Hesiod, on Mount Parnassus raised,
> With carefree, joyous voice and wondrous sweetness praised . . .

The speeches of Homer, on the other hand, Batyushkov translated in the high style, using the imagery of Russian odic poetry. One
of Homer's speeches is a paraphrase of certain famous lines of
Lomonosov. In the ode *The Year 1742,* Lomonosov wrote:

> There stallions with thunderous fetlocks
> *Vzdymayut k nebu prakh gustoy.*[42]
>
> There stallions with thunderous fetlocks
> Send thick dust billowing to the sky

Batyushkov's Homer says:

> *I koni burnye so zvonkoy kolesnitsey*
> *Pred ney ne budut prakh krutit'do oblakov.*[43]
>
> The thunderous stallions with their sounding chariot
> Before it will not churn the dust up to the clouds!

Millevoye says all this quite differently,[44] and Batyushkov's
text is much closer to Lomonosov's than to his French original.

Batyushkov's Homer is a poet in the lofty, civic tradition
of the high style; Hesiod—the elegiac poet of sentiment
and feeling. Batyushkov here presents the matter of his argument
against Olenin and Gnedich by showing us a poetic competition.
Here, it is quite immaterial which of the poets actually carries
off the laurels: the point is that they are represented as being of
equal merit, as talents of equal greatness. In this way, Batyushkov
was declaring the equality of all kinds, all genres of poetry in his
own age as well. Batyushkov's conviction did not accord with the
opinion of Gnedich and Olenin, but he chose to express it in the
elegant form of an elegy rather than in a critical article:

> And the Chalcide ruler, a weak king
> . . . . . . . . . . . . . . . . . . . . . . . . . . . . . . . .
>
> Did disregard the lofty hymn of deathless Homer
> And to his rival gave the palm of victory.
> Thus happy Hesiod received indemnity
> For songs inspired by that peace-loving Muse he served . . .[45]

Paradoxically, in Batyushkov's elegy Homer speaks of Hesiod's
poetry in a style approaching that of his rival; he seems to be mold-

ing his manner of poetic expression into a stylized imitation of manner proper to Hesiod:

> *Tvoy glas podobitsya amvrozii nebesnoy,*
> *Chto Geba yunaya sapfirnoy chashey l'ët*
> *Pevets! v ustakh tvoikh poezii prelestnoy*
> *Sladchayshiy Ol'miya blagoukhayet mëd.*[46]

> Thy voice is like celestial ambrosia poured
> By ever-youthful Hebe into sapphire cups
> Oh Singer! Sweeter still than fragrant honey stored
> At Olmius—the charm of poetry on the lips.

The equal right to existence of the elegy and of the ode, that is, the poetry of civic passions and political poetry, appeared from Batyushkov's point of view to be perfectly feasible because he saw the elegy itself as a genre of unlimited possibilities.

## IV  Use of Language in Poetry

In his *Discourse on the Influence of Light Verse on Language* (1816), Batyushkov developed his idea of equality between the genres, invoking the authority of Lomonosov: "This great founder of our literature knew and felt that the language of an enlightened people should satisfy all their requirements and not consist solely of high-flown words and expressions. He knew that, for all peoples ancient and modern, *light verse* which may be called the delightful extravagance of a literature, always occupies its own place of honor on Parnassus and is a constant source of fresh nourishment."[47]

At the same time, Batyushkov speaks of how much more exacting is the work of a poet in the lesser genres. He explains that "light verse" does not mean verse tossed off lightly but, on the contrary, makes extremely strict demands on the poet, compelling him to exercise a self-discipline unknown to the writer of epic or drama. "While the play is going on, what cold spectator will look for slips of style, when Polynices, robbed of crown and inner peace, throws himself in tears and despair at the feet of the wrathful Oedipus?"[48]

Batyushkov, presumably, had in mind the words of Polynices from Vladislav A. Ozerov's tragedy *Oedipus in Athens:*

> *Tvoy kayushchiysya syn padet k tvoim nogam . . .*[49]
>
> Behold your son repentant, prostrate at your feet . . .

Indeed, Ozerov's tragedy—the great success of the 1805–06 season, which Batyushkov must have remembered—had many grave defects in its lines, for instance, the comparison of "tears" to "torments," to which they are equal in "causticity."

In the tragedy, such defects could be compensated for by the acting and other resources at the disposal of the stage. The elegiac poet to whom Batyushkov is primarily referring, is alone with his reader; he will get away with nothing which goes to break the unity of the aesthetic impression. This is the completeness of the contact between the poet as a human being and his reader as a human being: "In the light type of verse the reader demands maximum perfection, purity of expression, harmony of language, subtlety, fluency; he demands sincerity of feeling and observance of the strictest decorum in every respect; he immediately becomes a severe judge, for his attention is not distracted in any way."[50]

Batyushkov understood "sincerity of feeling" as the natural desire of the reader to "see" what the poet described, to see—and thus to believe in—the true nature of the description. In fact, Batyushkov's independent work really began with his search for such a descriptive manner. For example, taking Parny's prose *Chansons Madécasses*: *"La danse est pour moi presque aussi douce qu'un baiser. Que vos pas soient lents, qu'ils imitent les attitudes du plaisir et l'abandon de la volupté,"*[51] Batyushkov turned it into verse:

> *Da tikhi, medlenny i strastny*
> *Telodvizhen'ya budut vnov',*
> *Da vsyudu, s chuvstvami soglasny,*
> *Yavlyayut negu i lyubov!*[52]
>
> Let slow, voluptuous, eloquent
> Of passion all your movements be,
> Let bodies' grace, with feelings blent,
> Show love and languid ecstasy.

This "blending" of the movements of the body with feelings, having nothing whatsoever to do with Parny's text, becomes one of the fundamental requirements Batyushkov makes of his own poetic style. "The movements of the body," that is, physical movement and physical states, must be shown—shown through the medium of words in all their dynamic mutability and in logical succession, not merely named as they had been before in the poetry of Russian Sentimentalism. The reader, it followed, was supposed to "see" these movements, the physical state of the characters described in his verse, and, judging by this state, to "divine" their feelings, to "blend" the movements of the body and the emotions they expressed.

In all his translations and adaptations Batyushkov replaced descriptions from the author's point of view by action and movement.

In a translation of one of Petrarch's sonnets, Batyushkov replaced the static picture given in the original by a description of eternally repeated action which is intended to express the full measure of the poet's sorrow for his dead mistress. Where Petrarch has:

> Che poss'io più, se no aver l'alma trista,
> Umidi gli occhi sempre e'l viso chino?[53]

Batyushkov writes:

> "Pochto zh mne dole zhit'?
> Uvy, chtob povtoryat' v chas polnochi rydan'ya
> I slëzy vechnye na khladny kamen' lit'!'[54]

> Why, why should I live on?
> Alas! Each night again to weep away the hours
> And shed eternal tears upon unresponsive stone.

In this way, Batyushkov uses the art of words to depict man in the outward expression of his inner state. It is quite different from the colorful word-painting we find in Derzhavin's works; Batyushkov uses words to show a definite, living situation in motion, not statically as painters would do. In a free translation which Batyushkov called an *Elegiya iz Tibulla* (*Elegy from Tibullus*), the scenes of Tibullus' separation from Delia and of his return are particularly characteristic of this manner of dynamic representation of episodes and situations.

Here is the scene of separation:

> *Chas gibel'nyy nastal*
> *I snova Deliya, pechal'na i unyla,*
> *Slezami polny vzor nevol'no obratila*
> *Na dal'ny put'. Ya sam, lishënny skorb'yu sil,*
> *"Utesh'sva"—Delii skvoz' slëzy govoril;*
> *"Utesh'sya!"—i eshchë s nevol'nym trepetan'em*
> *Pechal'nuyu lobzal poslednim lobyzan'em.*[55]

The dreadful hour had come,
And once more Delia, disconsolate, forlorn,
Reluctantly her tearful gaze did turn
Towards the distant road! I, too, weak from dismay,
"Take comfort," through my tears to Delia did say
"Take comfort," and, with trembling scarce suppressed,
My sad love with a farewell kiss I kissed.

In this passage, there is not a word of comment from the author and, with the exception of the description of Delia as *pechal'na i unyla* ("disconsolate, forlorn") there is no naming of sentiments, no attempt to define the hero's inward state. Everything has been translated into dynamic action—gesture and movement—into a dramatic scene filled with a genuine sense of tragedy.

In quite a different tone, but just as visually by a sequence of actions and movements, Batyushkov describes the final episode in the same elegy, that of Delia awaiting her husband and his homecoming:

> Beneath your sheltered roof, when winter winds bring snow,
> Your friend in the dark night will set her lamp aglow,
> And, slowly twirling round the spindle in her hands,
> Will tell fair tales of olden times and far-off lands
> And you will lend your ear to those sweet, foolish fables,
> Will lose yourself in dream, my friend, and, scarcely able
> To prop up closing lids, your distaff to the floor
> Let drop . . . but see—your man is standing at the door.[56]

This scene showing how Delia spends her time during the separation is an insertion of Batyushkov's own; there is nothing remotely reminiscent of this episode in Tibullus.

As L. S. Fleyshman has rightly pointed out: "The elegy's launching into the mainstream of Russian poetry should be dated not to 1802, the year of the publication of the elegies of

Zhukovsky *In a Country Churchyard* and of Andrey Turgenev
*Sullen Autumn's deadening hand...* (*Ugryumoy oseni mert-
vyashchaya ruka...*), but from somewhere around the middle
of the 1810's."[57] Further, he established a well-founded connection
between his "launching" of the elegy and Batyushkov's works.
"The pages of literary journals are filled with theoretical, original
and translated, articles on the elegy. Batyushkov brought out his
literary manifesto, proving the poetic and social significance of
the lesser poetic genres."[58] This manifesto, the *Discourse on the
Influence of Light Verse on Language,* had evidently been written
at the beginning of 1816. In it, Batyushkov drew his conclusions
from his own experience of work on the creation of new genres
in Russian poetry, especially, the elegy. By the time he wrote his
*Discourse,* Batyushkov was already the author of a number of
fine original elegies *The Shade of a Friend, Separation, Tavrida,
Hope, To a Friend* and a number of epistolary verses, developing
the style of *My Penates.* For this reason, it is better to examine
Batyushkov's system of opinions after an analysis of his elegiac
poetry in the form it had attained by the beginning of 1816.

## V  *The Elegiac Manner*

In the elegies of 1814–15 Batyushkov's art attained full maturity.
He understood this himself and found it possible to begin preparing
a book of poems, for he now firmly believed that he had a significant contribution to make to Russian poetry.

In *Tavrida,*—according to Pushkin, the author's own favorite
poem—Batyushkov uses his elegiac manner with perfect freedom
and apparent spontaneity. Those difficulties which Batyushkov
had when working out his elegiac style were overcome in *Tavrida.*
Here he finds that harmony which he had always sought between
what he had to express and its stylistic incarnation. In the lyrical
*personae,* the elegiac "I's" addressed to his beloved, Batyushkov
employed the same technique of expressing the mental and
sentimental through the physical and the psychological state
through movement and gesture:

> *O, radost'! Ty so mnoy vstrechayesh' solntsa svet
> I, lozhe schastiya s dennitsey pokidaya,*

*Rumyana i svezha, kak roza polevaya,*
*So mnoyu delish' trud, zaboty i obed.*
*So mnoy v chas vechera, pod krovom tikhoy nochi*
*So mnoy, vsegda so mnoy; tvoi prelestny ochi*
*Ya vizhu, golos tvoy ya slyshu,* i ruka
V tvoey pokoitsya vsechasno.[59]

Oh rapture! You and I together wake to greet
The sun and rise with it from our sweet, shared repose,
You blooming fresh and fair as the wild briar rose;
Together we do share our work, our cares, our meat,
Together as night falls, and all the gentle night
Together, always with me; your dear eyes alight
With loveliness I see, and hear your voice; *my hand*
*In yours does rest at all times.*

This detailed account of a country day, not disdaining to mention even a shared dinner, is something that would appear quite out of place in Parny's elegies, for example, but here it is transformed into a powerful and poignant crescendo of feeling by the anaphoristic "So mnoy ..." ("Together ... "). As was Batyushkov's invariable custom, he did not once name this feeling in *Tavrida,* but the entire exposition evokes it—the description of the changing seasons and the landscape of the "Southern land"—the Crimea-Tavrida as imagined by Batyushkov.

The dynamics of Batyushkov's elegies are not dictated solely by the subject, but also by the contents, that is, by a peculiar, elegiac conception of time.

Batyushkov wrote his elegies both as heir to the traditions of Russian eighteenth-century poetry and as their destroyer, as an innovator. In the poetry of Russian eighteenth-century Classicism, each genre had its own particular conception of time, its attitude to time, and its way of conveying it. Time in the plot is usually a transition from the time of the initial situation, conventionally placed in the past, to the present, that is, to the time in which the action of the story is taking place. As a rule, the action of the story is simultaneous with the moment of narration. In any case, the trend of story-time is toward coincidence, synchronization of the event and its narration. In the solemn ode, the poetical genre particularly characteristic of the eighteenth century, there is usually an awareness of two times—the past, more often than not of the preceding reign, and of a new epoch which has replaced it. From the point of view of the odic poet, this new reign has many advantages, since it has already achieved a definite cycle of reforms or measures beneficial to the common weal and is capable of achieving still more in the future. Odic time is historical time, presupposing a succession of historical epochs and affirming the dependence of this succession on political events, more often than not, on a change of monarch.

The elegy's relationship to time is unique, quite different from that of the ode or the fable. The theoreticians of the elegy who were usually its practitioners, saw the basic function of the genre as the depiction of the contradictory complexity of man's emotions. Millevoye, whose poetry Batyushkov knew well and had translated, in his preface to his *Collected Works* entitled "On the Elegy," wrote: "Even when we sing of happiness it may preserve the taint of sorrow which belongs to it. A mixture of contrasting impressions heightens the effect."[60]

Formulated in such general terms this definition was accepted by many, but the stumbling block to achieving it in practice was the difficulty of finding new stylistic means for embracing this "mixture of contrasting impressions."

The first poem in the first book of Millevoye's *Elegies* was *La Chute des feuilles,* his best known elegy, and one Batyushkov chose for adaptation. In Millevoye, the lyrical subject is built up on the parallel between autumn, the dying of nature, and the foreboding of death in the soul of the young poet—a foreboding which proves fully justified. The poet dies and is forgotten. The elegy is written in the form of a monologue pronounced by the poet, his regrets at his own inevitable death, preceded by a brief evocation of autumn. It culminates in a description of his own lonely grave.

In Millevoye's *Collected Works* there are three versions of this elegy; two in the text, one in the notes. The most significant change Millevoye made in the second version was that the poet's mother, albeit seldom, visits his grave, whereas in the first version of the basic text the peace of his grave is disturbed only by "the shepherd from the valley." Batyushkov did not accept this alteration; moreover, he omitted all mention of the mother in the poet's monologue; the hero of his verse longs only for his beloved Delia and for his friends. Presumably, the mention of the mother seemed to Batyushkov redundant and sentimental.

He also fundamentally rearranged the basic lyrical situation. Batyushkov's elegy is set against a background of spring, not autumn as is Millevoye's. Therefore, instead of the parallel between the poet's death and the autumnal dying of Nature, there is the contrast between her vernal blossoming and the death of the young poet, "the bard of love." In accordance with this change, Batyushkov's poem is called *The Last Spring* (*Poslednyaya vesna*).

The contrast between the burgeoning of spring and the fading of the hero is maintained throughout the poem:

> *V polyakh blistaet may* vesëly!
> *Ruchey* svobodno *zazhurchal,*
> *I* yarkiy *golos Filomely*
> *Ugryumy bor ocharoval:*
> *Vsë* novoy *zhizni p'ët dykhan'e!*
> *Pevets lyubvi, lish' ty unyl!*
> *Ty smerti vernoy predveshchan'e*
> *V pechal'nom serdtse zaklyuchil*
> ...............................................
> *Zazeleneyut gibki lozy,*
> *Polya odenutsya v tsvety,*
> *Tam* pervye *uvidish' rozy,*
> *I s nimi vdrug uvyanesh' ty.*[61]

> *Bright* May has set the field ablaze!
> *Untrammelled* rush the gurgling rills,
> The gloomy pinewood stands amazed
> At Philomela's *vivid* trills.
> All things breathe deep *new* life's fresh morning!
> Yet, bard of love, you stand apart!
> Alone, oppressed by sure forewarning
> Of death close-locked in your sad heart.
> . . . . . . . . . . . . . . . . . . . . . . . .
> When supple shoot its green discloses
> And meadows don their floweriest dress,
> Then you will see the *first* red roses—
> And with them fade into the grass.

The dissimilarity of feelings in Batyushkov's adaptation is achieved by the basic contrast between spring and death, by the

choice of particularly expressive epithets designed to drive home
this thematic contrast, and by the consequential changes of verb
tense.

In the excerpt from *The Last Spring* just quoted, the italicized
epithets are all introduced by Batyushkov, Millevoye having no
need of them, for he describes autumn, not spring. The words
these epithets are made to qualify are, as a rule, also selected on
a contrasting principle, so that the couplings of adjective and noun
are often strikingly unexpected. One cannot explain such phrases
as "yarkiy golos Filomely" ("Philomela's vivid trills") simply by
the poet's desire to convey an impression of the fullness of life,
of its joyful burgeoning, the better to set off the bitter lot of the
youthful poet.

In one of his articles written in 1815, Batyushkov wrote: "Let
us in passing call the attention of poets to how great a force
the most ordinary words obtain when used in the right place,"
and immediately supported this statement by a quotation from
Lomonosov's tragedy *Tamira and Selim,* underlining the verbs.[62]
It was the verbs, the way they were placed, their deliberate subordi-
nation, that Batyushkov wished to emphasize. In his work on the
elegies of 1814–16, Batyushkov created his system of placing verbs
in relation to the general movement of the elegiac subject, of its
contrasting shifts of tense and mood. A good example of this is
the elegy *Convalescence, (Vyzdorovlenie)* according to Pushkin,
"one of the best" in Batyushkov's poetry.[63] It was first printed
in *Essays* and was an entirely reworked version of the autobiographical episode recounted in the original version of the elegy under
the title *Reminiscences of 1807.* In verse structure and style, it
closely resembles Batyushkov's 1815–16 elegies, thus there is no
foundation for dating it between 1807 and 1809, as some students
of Batyushkov's poetry still do.

In this elegy, the poet, by means of clearly marked and well-
thought-out variation of verb tense together with firm, precise
composition, manages to find expression for a very complex
sequence of emotional states through the physically expressed
emotions of man:

> *Kak landysh pod serpom ubiystvennym zhnetsa*
> *Sklonyaet golovu i vyanet;*
> *Tak ya v bolezni zhdal bezvremenno kontsa*

> I dumal: parki chas nastanet.
> Uzh ochi pokryval Ereba mrak gustoy,
>    Uzh serdtse medlennee bilos':
> Ya vyanul, ischezal, i zhizni molodoy,
>    Kazalos', solntse zakatilos'.
> No ty priblizhilas', o zhizn' dushi moey,
>    I alykh ust tvoikh dykhan'e,
> I slëzy plamenem sverkayushchikh ochey,
>    I potseluev sochetan'e,
> I vzdokhi strastnye, i sila milykh slov
>    Menya iz oblasti pechali,
> Ot Orkovykh poley, ot Lety beregov
> Dlya sladostrastiya prizvali.
> Ty snova zhizn' daësh'; ona tvoy dar blagoy,
>    Toboy dyshat' do groba stanu.
> Mne sladok budet chas i muki rokovoy:
>    Ya ot lyubvi teper' uvyanu.[64]

As a frail floweret before the deadly scythe
   Will meekly bow its head and languish,
So I in sickness thought: there is no hope of life,
   Soon now will fall the stroke of anguish.
Already Erebus' dense darkness covered me,
   Already my heart slowed to rest:
I was dissolving, fading; young life's sun in me
   It seemed had sunk beyond the West:
But then you came to me, ah dear life of my heart,
   And your red lips' quiet breathing
And ardent tears that in your eyes did start,
   And your warm kisses cleaving,
And sighs of passion, and the might of amiable words
   From the cold vale of sadness
From Orcus' fields and Lethe's dreadful shores
   Did summon me to love and gladness.
You gave me life anew; it is your blessed gift.
   Till death, my life shall be thanksgiving.
For me, the hour of mortal anguish will be bliss;
   For I shall languish now from loving.

   Very striking in this elegy is the precision and lucidity of the composition, the balance of all its elements.

Consisting of twenty lines, the first eight expound the initial situation: the hero's sickness and expectation of death. In the next eight lines (9–16) we have the appearance of the beloved and a favorable change in the condition of the "patient."

Thus, the first eight lines are devoted to the hero, the following eight to the heroine; the last four lines unite the lovers and, at the same time, synthesize the two themes of sickness and convalescence.

The distribution of time in *Convalescence* is strictly subordinated to a definite order dictated by the lyrical subject. The first two lines containing the lily of the valley (floweret) simile are essentially outside time and are therefore given in the present tense (*sklonyaet . . . vyanet,* "will bow . . . languish," "will" denotes habit, not futurity); lines 3–8 are in the past tense, for they tell of an action already concluded, of the "sickness" of the hero which began long ago and already nearing a sorry end in his final demise. Therefore, in the eighth line, concluding this part of the verse and the theme of sickness, the imperfective aspect of the verbs (*dumal, pokryval bilos', vyanul, ischezal:* thought, covered, was beating, was dissolving, fading) is replaced by the perfective of result: *zakatilos'* (had sunk).

The adversative conjunction "but" in the ninth line divides the two parts of the poem from one another, the part about *him,* from the part (lines 9–16) about *her.* This part of the elegy, in contrast to the first part, is constructed as one long period almost without verbs, entirely composed of nominative combinations. Verbs begin and end this excerpt: "*No ty priblizhilas' . . . dlya sladostrastiya prizvali.*" ("But then you came . . . did summon me to love and gladness.") The last verb concludes a period of deliberately piled up adverbial-nominative clauses. Their accumulative effect lends a particular power, a supercharged emotional force to the final verb "prizvali." The fact that the verbs in this part are in the past tense is legitimate, since all this, too, happened some time ago, before the beginning of the *action* of the elegy, that is, before the "resurrection" and "healing" of the sick poet. At the moment when the action begins the past tense is replaced by the present.

Once the "resurrection" had taken place and the sick poet is healed, he may believe in the permanence of possible happiness, and the present tense yields to the future.

The final three lines bring us back to the beginning, to the theme of death, but already overcome by love, transformed from a real threat, from death in the literal sense of the word, into a metaphor which now unites love and death in a single sentiment.

While, in *Convalescence* the movement of the lyrical subject in time is given in an abstract form emancipated from biographical or historical sequence, the elegy *To a Friend* is an attempt to give us the history of the hero's inner life, changes of opinions, and successions of moral criteria. The hero of the latter elegy, in whose name the whole sequence of ideas is expounded, takes his point of departure from the particular incident of the destruction of a friend's house and the death of his beloved, and goes on to give a general assessment of life expressing his own doubts of the possibility of understanding either the course of human destinies or the laws of history. He renews his earlier attitude to reality and seeks comfort in religion.

Batyushkov devoted the elegy *Hope* to the same theme: the reevaluation of moral criteria.

However, in *To a Friend,* this theme is worked out more fully. Batyushkov was as specific as he possibly could be about the general, historical premises governing individual fates. The destruction of the "house" is also the destruction—or, at best, the crisis—of a personal philosophy, the collapse of a whole era of thought, of a vast sphere of ideas on which the poet, his friend, and many other former habitués of the "house" had based their whole way of life.

> *Gde dom tvoy, schast'ya dom? . . . on v bure bed ischez,*
> *I mesto proroslo krapivoy . . .* [65]

> Where is your joyous house? . . . Gone in a storm of ills,
> The site now overgrown with nettles . . .

The "house" in the context of this elegy has a quite different significance to that which in *My Penates* is described by so many synonyms for a poet's dwelling: cloister, hovel, shack, cot, little house. Not one of these words has any claim to be considered a real description, for all are intended to emphasize that the action of *My Penates* takes place not so much "in the country near Moscow" as in the land of poetic fancy which is the poet's home.

The "house" in *To a Friend* is a real house, the dwelling of the person to whom the elegy is addressed. This house is destroyed in war, most probably in the Moscow fire of 1812, although the poem does not in fact provide us with sufficient data to license such speculation. "House" is not a word used as a mere conventional appellation for the abstract habitation of a poet. Yet, at the same time, it is not simply a house which stands or stood in a street and fulfilled its direct function as a man's dwelling place. In Batyushkov's poem it is a "joyous house," a whole sphere of life and thought, that land of happiness where the master of the house and his kindred souls found rest and shelter.

From a real designation of an ordinary object of everyday use, this house is transformed into a poetic symbol for the beautiful, the joyous, and the hopelessly lost—a symbol of youth and beauty which are gone, never to return.

A similar transformation, yet with full retention of objective meaning, is undergone by all the concepts and designation introduced into the poem. Moreover, this double meaning makes possible combinations of words and concepts of very different stylistic and cultural provenance:

> *No gde minutny shum vesel'ya i pirov?*
> *V vine potoplennye chashi?*
> *Gde mudrost' svetskaya siyayushchikh umov?*
> *Gde tvoy Falern i rozy nashi?*[66]

> Where is the short-lived stir of feasts and gaiety?
> The cup that brimming wine encloses?
> Where are the brilliant minds, the subtle sophistry?
> Where your Falerno and our roses?

The combination of poetic concepts in the last line is very typical of the general tendency toward symbolic transformation of real objects, even of names.[67] "Falerno," the name of a wine loved by Horace, is transformed into a symbolic appellation of wine in general; next to it stands the word "roses," apparently quite free of any ulterior significance and serving simply to designate a kind of flower. Yet Falerno and roses are presented as antitheses; they are contrasted: "Your Falerno" and "our roses." From a designation for wine, Falerno is transformed into a symbol for feasting, hospitality, and friendship, in a word—everything beautiful that came from the master of the house; whereas "our roses" are transformed into a poetic symbol of the feelings and sentiments presented by the friends to the master of the house as their contribution to the feast of life.

This system of word usage, wherein a word goes beyond its objective meaning and is transformed into a generalized philosophical designation for a wide sphere of concepts and ideas, is applied by Batyushkov equally to all verbal material of his elegies. This use of the word as a condenser of meanings related to highly important fields of contemporary thinking allows Batyushkov to make bold combinations of words and to produce unexpected semantic effects, not only in the sphere of concrete meanings, but, more importantly, in the field of abstract concepts, particularly in the world of ethic and aesthetic principles. Batyushkov becomes so free in his combinations of words that he can juxtapose them on a basis of very remote association.

> *Minutny stranniki, my khodim po grobam*
> Pilgrims of one minute's span, we walk on dead men's graves

In this line, one should not think of a direct interpretation of either part: "Minutny" ("of the minute") in combination with "stranniki" ("pilgrims") conveys the brevity of man's sojourn on earth, the brevity of human life in general; the word "minutny" is chosen, most probably, just because it is so concrete. This word is almost a technical, special term taken from the lexical store which had established the clock as the emblem and symbol of time in all European poetry since the Renaissance. In combination with the word "stranniki," however, the word "minutny" acquires a certain quality of length, as going on a pilgrimage is necessarily a process, a continuous action in time, and not something which is accomplished at once. This pilgrimage or wandering is made a function of the whole of humanity by the use of the pronoun "we" in the poet's monologue; all of "us," all people in their brief earthly pilgrimage, tread the earth which harbors the graves (i.e., the mortal remains) of countless generations of our fellows. Thus the bold metonymy "my khodim po grobam" (we walk on graves) by virtue of its very deliberate, even slightly shocking, profane, concrete nature, becomes a poetic generalization of tremendous semantic capacity. "Light" poetry becomes far from light; it no longer resolves the fundamental problems of human existence ("the secrets of eternity and the grave") in that optimistic, offhand fashion in which it resolved them in *My Penates.* Within its scope are now such complex problems as the staging of a drama of the spirit, as a change of philosophical direction. *To a Friend,* in the condensed form of an elegy, expounds the contents of a drama of ideas, of a great philosophical drama. What in Zhukovsky's poetry is always the keynote, the main, all conquering idea—the superiority of the ideal world to the real, the imperfections of life on Earth and the unattainability of happiness—appears in Batyushkov's poetry as the climax of a certain process of spiritual inquiry, as the finale of a lyrical drama, as a kind of catharsis.

Time, in Batyushkov's elegies of 1814 to 1817, ceases to be something abstract—a mere convention—as it is, for example, in the odes of Derzhavin. The majority of Derzhavin's odes, even those like *On the Death of Meshchersky* (*Na smert' Meshcherskogo*), *On Happiness* (*Na schastie*), *Life at Zvanskoe* (*Zhizn' Zvanskaya*) the whole philosophic import of which is in depicting the mutability, "the treacherousness" of human destiny, do not contain in their inner structure any indications of the role of time in the fate of the individual. For Batyushkov, the fundamental ethico-philosophical problem to which he is seeking a solution lies in the relationship between time and eternity. Time is the process of history, the march of events in which every man plays his part. It is the sphere in which he may find himself in the role of a hero or a victim, but it is one in which he lives and acts, whether or not this be his will or his desire. Eternity is the whole life of humanity above and outside history; eternity is the sphere of the triumph of the ideal principles of morality or religion. Only communion with this world of eternal moral categories can bring happiness. But how is such a communion possible? When he wrote his most mature works, Batyushkov considered that all philosophical systems heretofore invented give only partial answers, all are but relatively true. Absolute truth, the full answer, it seems to him, can only be given by religion based on eternal, unfading categories. This assertion of the immutable validity of religion closes his elegy *To a Friend:*

> In fear at last I counsel of my conscience sought . . .
> The darkness cleared, mine eyes could see,

> And Faith her saving oil to Hope's lampad did bring
> And filled it full with light for me.
>
> It seemed the sun had drenched my graveward road in light . . .
> Firm-footed onward now I tread,
> And for a better world my spirit shall take flight,
> My dusty pilgrim's garment shed.[68]

In the last verse, the pilgrim theme and the death theme are reintroduced, the last in an unusual, almost unnatural combination with the theme of light and sun.

The poet's thought wells up, as it were, from the confluence of the temporal life of man with the world of eternal truths. What we have here is a spiritual transformation of human consciousness, and the hero of the verse is actually in process of becoming a different person. For the first time in Russian poetry the changing of a man within time—the life of the soul as a process, as movement from one way of thinking and feeling to another different way—becomes the subject of poetry, in which the spiritual life of contemporary man was to dictate the nature of the basic conflict and the ways in which it was to be resolved. In the first real Romantic poem by Alexander Pushkin, the *Prisoner of the Caucasus* (*Kavkazsky plennik*, 1821) "the hero may be considered as the mouthpiece of the contemporary elegy."[69]

Pushkin achieved a unity which, in Batyushkov's elegies, still remained just beyond reach; that is, he found that sphere where all human problems, eternal and temporal, commingle. In Pushkin's poetry, the sphere where all ways meet might be defined as contemporary history filtered through the spiritual consciousness of the thinking man of his own generation.

Batyushkov's elegies constituted a first but extremely important step toward this synthesis of philosophy and history in literature which, until his time, had been confined to separate spheres.

### CHAPTER 6

# Essays in Verse and Prose *and After* Essays

## I  *Essays, Volume One*

O N his return from the wars, Batyushkov again became absorbed in literary interests. The animation of Russian society following the victories over Napoleon found expression in a sharp politico-philosophical controversy in which Batyushkov's Petersburg friends and acquaintances took the liveliest interest. One of his close acquaintances, Sergey Semyonovich Uvarov, left us the following characterization of Russian society at the end of 1813:

> The confusion is unbounded. Some want harmless enlightenment, that is fire which will not burn: others, and they are the majority, hold Napoleon and Montesquieu, the French armies and French books ... the ravings of Shishkov and the discoveries of Leibnitz to be all of a piece; in a word, there is such a chaos of loud speaking, passions, bitterly opposed parties and one-sided exaggerations that to contemplate the spectacle for any length of time is quite unbearable. People fling the most violent phrases at one another: "religion is threatened," "the shattering of morality," "advocate of foreign ideas," "luminary," "philosopher," "Freemason," "fanatic," etc. In a word, total confusion.[1]

Batyushkov was carried away by this atmosphere of debate, moral stock-taking, and reappraisal. In 1814–15 he wrote many philosophical tracts and critical articles in prose. A convinced supporter of gradual reform as the best way of social progress, Batyushkov at that time still shared the hopes of liberally-inclined, educated Russians for the possibility of abolishing serfdom in Russia on the initiative of the government. According to Vyazemsky, in 1814 Batyushkov even composed "a fine quatrain in which, addressing the Emperor Alexander, he said that after the conclusion of the glorious war to liberate Europe the Emperor was called by Providence to perfect his fame and immortalize his reign by the liberation of the Russian people."[2] This lost quatrain was, however, Batyushkov's only political statement in verse. His faith in enlightenment as the surest way to social progress was expounded in his prose articles, particularly in *An Evening with Kantemir* (1816).

Now Batyushkov decided that the time was ripe to publish a collection of his works. He was persuaded of this by his own instinct and by the unconditional approval of his friends, particularly of Zhukovsky who had the highest opinion of the elegies written in the second half of 1815 in Kamenets-Podolsk, where Batyushkov was still stationed with the army. At the beginning of 1816, he retired from the army and moved to Moscow where he settled down to preparing the two volumes of his collected works, finally published in the autumn of 1817 under the title *Essays in Verse and Prose by Konstantin Batyushkov.* Part I contained his prose articles and translations; Part II, his poetry.

The combination of prose and poetry in one collection was not in itself a novelty for Russian literature, although, as a rule, poets made separate publications of verse only. Batyushkov evidently attached serious importance to his prose. This is clear from the fact that for *Essays* he reworked his satirical article *A Discourse in Praise of Sleep* (*Pokhval'noe slovo snu,* first published in 1810), providing a new preface and including a satirical portrait of the alleged author. All the other articles which came out in the first volume of *Essays*, Batyushkov also subjected to careful corrections and some alterations.

The actual arrangement of the articles in this volume shows that Batyushkov was anxious to leave his reader with a definite impression. The volume opens with the "Discourse on the Influence of Light Verse on Language" and the article "A Word on Poetry and the Poet," key works in which Batyushkov expounded his basic thoughts on the problems which he believed confronted contemporary Russian poetry. These are followed by three articles about Russian poets (Lomonosov, Kantemir, and Muraviev) and an article on modern Russian painting ("A Stroll Through the Academy of Arts"). The articles on Italian poets ("Ariosto and Tasso," "Petrarch") are placed together with a translation from Boccaccio ("Griselda"), and the volume is concluded with articles of general philosophical content: "On the Best Qualities of the Heart" (O luchshikh svoystvakh serdtsa) and "A Word on Morality, Based on Philosophy and Religion" (Nechto o morali, osnovannoy na filosofii i religii).

While concurring with Buffon, the French eighteenth-century scientist and stylist, that *"le style est l'homme même,"* Batyushkov could not be content with reaching a conclusion on the psyche of the poet by applying Buffon's truism to the works of Lomonosov. "Without doubt," he asserted "we may conclude from Lomonosov's prose and verse that he was a man of high soul, clear and penetrating mind, and uncommonly strong, enterprising character."[3] All this seemed to Batyushkov a true but insufficient, incomplete, and one-sided depiction of the character of the poet.

Batyushkov, a man of the Romantic era, wanted to picture Lomonosov in all his complexity, to see behind the work of the poet of the mid-eighteenth century his character as a person and, in this, to find the key to his poetry. "The lover of literature," he argues against Buffon,

I will go further, the philosophically inclined observer, would like to know certain details about the private life of the great man, to get to know him, to discover his passions, his anxieties, his sorrows, pleasures, habits, eccentricities, weaknesses, and even his vices, those inescapable companions of mankind.[4]

In contrast to the official eulogies in praise of Lomonosov, Batyushkov perceived in him a live, passionate nature whose actions were conceived in "a fiery heart." The life and work of Lomonosov were for him the offspring of the poet's "sensibility," of his "fiery imagination," that is, of his capacity for a lively reaction to events and for finding an original poetic form in which to describe them. Such is Lomonosov in the imagination of Batyushkov, quite a different person from the academician and dry court poet into which the zealots of the old literature had transformed him.

The first volume of Batyushkov's *Essays,* deeply impregnated with those ideas and conceptions of poetry which were only partially expressed in the article on Lomonosov, prepared the reader for the second volume, where he would enter the world of the poet's own verses. In the poem *To My Friends,* with which volume two opens, the author offers his reader:

> *Istoriyu moikh strastey,*
> *Uma serdtsa zabluzhden'ya,*
> *Zaboty, suety, pechali prezhnikh dney*
> *I legkokryly naslazhden'ya.*[5]

The story of my passions here,
Of mind and heart the wayward errors,
The cares, the vanities, the griefs of yesteryear
And its light-winged pleasures . . .


## II   *Criticism of* Essays

The publication of *Essays* was facilitated by Gnedich. The correspondence between the poets showed that Batyushkov was very concerned both about the text and the choice of poems for the second volume. Some of his early poems he excluded from *Essays* altogether, others he reworked, occasionally making substantial alterations. He sought the opinions of Zhukovsky, Vyazemsky, and particularly Gnedich in preparing the text of the poems for publication.

Batyushkov's alterations were not always approved by his friends or by the readers of *Essays*. For instance, Gnedich and, later Pushkin, preferred the earlier version of a line in the translation of *Tibullus' Elegy*. Originally Batyushkov had:

> *O podvigakh svoikh rasskazhet drevniy voin,*
> *Tovarishch yunosti, i, sidya za stolom,*
> *Pust' ratny stan chertit chash prolitykh vinom.*[6]

> Some grizzled soldier will recount his bygone exploits,
> Some comrade of my youth; and, sitting at my table,
> In wine from spilt cups trace the ordering of battle.

In *Essays* Batyushkov altered the last line to:

> *Mne lager' nachertit veselykh chash vinom.*
> In wine from jocose cups will trace his camp embattled.

The reason for this change evidently lay in the poet's desire to increase the emotional impact of the line. Therefore, he replaced the precise, concrete word "spilt" by the epithet "jocose," unexpected in the context and, by virtue of its unexpectedness, lending the entire exposition a different character, putting it into a different emotional key.

After almost a year's preparatory work, *Essays in Verse and Prose* appeared in print. Only then did the educated public have its first opportunity to judge and appraise all that Batyushkov had accomplished and to try to define his place in Russian poetry.

In an attempt to comfort Batyushkov when he was already suffering from a serious psychological condition, Gnedich wrote to him in 1821 that he was

a uniquely fortunate fellow whom, from his first step onto the literary arena, criticism has not dared to touch, a poet who bears on his brow all the signs of Apollo's favor, who began to acquire in youth and did acquire while still young what others obtain only after having made it a lifetime goal: general respect and general acknowledgment of his fine talent and his contribution to literature.[7]

As it happened, Gnedich wrote no more than the truth. In 1817, the year of publication, critics greeted *Essays in Verse and Prose* with praise. The fundamental thought which all the reviews shared is that Batyushkov had already for many years occupied one of the first places in Russian poetry. Sergey Glinka wrote: "Konstantin Batyushkov's verses not only enjoy considerable renown, but many know them by heart." A. E. Izmaylov called him "one of our best and most Classic poets."[8] V. Kozlov expressed the same thought with oratorial pathos: "Who among the enlightened lovers of the literature of our fatherland has not read, has not been enchanted by the verses of Mr. Batyushkov? Who has not seen in him one of the most worthy poets of the Alexandrine age?"[9] Grech also placed Batyushkov in the first rank of contemporary poets:

Among the works of Russian authors published over the last year the first place is occupied by K. N. Batyushkov's *Essays in Verse and Prose.* The rich imagination, ardent feeling, new bold thoughts together with a charming vivacity, lightness, and exemplary correctness of style are the merits of Mr. Batyushkov's works, and these qualities ensure him a place *in the first rank* of our writers.[10]

It must be added that Batyushkov's prose, in spite of his own doubts, enjoyed as great a success as his poetry.

The most serious reaction to *Essays* was an article by Sergey Uvarov in which he unambiguously stated that Batyushkov and Zhukovsky represented *a new school* of Russian literature, a school formed at the beginning of the nineteenth century which had replaced the *old school* formed in the eighteenth century.

At the same time Uvarov, who allotted Zhukovsky the first place in Russian literature, considered that Batyushkov's significance could be assessed only in comparison with Zhukovsky's. This alone must have been extremely gratifying to Batyushkov. After Derzhavin's recent death in 1816 only he and Zhukovsky could be considered as poets who had made a significant contribution to the development of Russian literature. Uvarov wrote:

Among the new writers, it is Mr. Zhukovsky who occupies the first place.... The poet of 1812 is the favorite of the nation. While acknowledging the excellence of his talent and his undoubted right to preeminence, connoisseurs have so far failed definitely to appoint a suitable place to Mr. Batyushkov.... Batyushkov and Zhukovsky are alike only insofar as both feel the beauty of their mother tongue, both are gifted with brilliant imagination and perfect harmony; but in all else they follow different paths, and for this reason the talent of the one cannot be ranked lower than the talent of the other.[11]

Uvarov goes on to give an outline of the individual peculiarities of each poet and in doing so makes use of a technique often employed by critics of that time and still employed in the mid-1820's: the comparison of a Russian with a foreign poet. This device made it possible to point out the newness for Russian poetry of certain themes and images of the poet, and, at the same time, to establish his connection with the general movement of contemporary literature. Uvarov had yet another aim in mind when he pointed out in his article the difference between the literary sources of inspiration of Zhukovsky and Batyushkov. He wanted to make it clear to Batyushkov's readers that the Russian poet had quite broken with previous literary tradition and that not the French seventeenth or eighteenth century classics, like Racine and Voltaire, but the elegiac poets of ancient and modern times had been his literary mentors: "Zhukovsky, nourished on the English and German writers, has become our Scott, our Lord Byron, our Goethe, whereas Batyushkov, a passionate lover of Italian and French poetry, imitates that which is *molle atque facetum* in the former, and those most moving delights which distinguish the latter."[12]

Having defined the various literary orientations of Zhukovsky and Batyushkov, Uvarov turns to an analysis of their poetic manners:

One has more power, more movement, the other more elegance and polish. . . . One is a poet of the North, the other—of the South. Zhukovsky's colors are vivid and pictorial; his style glitters with tropes; a living and profound sensibility animates all his works. Batyushkov is more smooth, more correct, more careful of bold departures from the conventional; his taste is mature, he is passionate rather than sentimental; he is equally successful in his imitations of Tibullus and Parny.[13]

The success of *Essays* with critics, fellow-writers, and readers was naturally extremely gratifying to Batyushkov and lulled for a time his everlasting doubt of himself and of his gifts, but not for long.

### III   *Work on Volume II*

Soon after the publication of *Essays,* Batyushkov wrote Gnedich that he was not satisfied with the book. He wanted to "revise and rewrite it all . . ."[14]

Batyushkov's dissatisfaction with his collection evidently had many different causes, and it is impossible to reconstruct them all. There are, however, some foundations for the assumption that one of the causes may have been the author's dissatisfaction with the disparity between the "content" of the volume of verse and the interpretation which the poet himself wished to be made of that content. In Gnedich's introduction to the second volume of *Essays* there was a passage which read:

We must warn the lovers of literature that the greater part of these verses was written before the essays in prose, at different times, amid the racket of military camps or during snatched moments of wartime relaxation, but we have not thought it necessary to indicate the time and circumstances of each poem's writing. The publisher hopes that the readers themselves will easily distinguish the later from the earlier works and find in them more maturity of thought and greater discrimination in the choice of subjects.[15]

Allowing himself to be guided by these requirements—"maturity of thought" and "greater discrimination in the choice of subjects"— Batyushkov had not only excluded from the *Essays* his unpublished earlier works, but also everything published in 1809 and some of his 1810 publications, including translations from Petrarch, Parny's *Chansons Madécasses,* La Fontaine's fable *Philomela and Procne,* and a number of epigrammatic trifles. *A Vision on*

*the Shores of the Lethe* was not included in *Essays* either, probably for reasons of censorship: Batyushkov may have feared that the
personal satire on Shishkov would awake doubts on the part of the
publishers. A considerable part of those pieces not included in
*Essays* is made up of epigrams and "occasional verses." Batyushkov might well have considered these dated and not reprinted
them for that reason. On the whole, the selection of verses tended
to give the collection unity of mood, and Batyushkov followed
this principle strictly, particularly in the most important part of
the book, the section devoted to the elegy.

In the poem *To My Friends,* which Batyushkov had written
in 1815, he defined the general content of the collection: *I, slovom,
ves' zhurnal/Zdes' druzhestvo naydët bespechnogo poeta . . .*[16] In
short, friendship will find/Herein the diary of the carefree poet.

Batyushkov seems to have had no definite guiding principle in
his arrangement of elegies within the section. "I would advise you
to put the elegies at the beginning," he wrote to Gnedich; "first,
those which please you more, then those that are not so good, and
the best last. Just as a regiment is formed. The poor soldiers in the
middle."[17] He also made cuts in some poems in which there
was a preponderance of real biographical material, rejecting these
passages. In this way, the elegy *Recollections of 1807,* the full text
of which runs to 102 lines, Batyushkov printed in *Essays* in ab-
breviated form (43 lines), omitting the entire story of his happy
love. Another elegy, *Memories,* subtitled *A Fragment,* was originally 32 lines longer. To what was said in the basic part of that
elegy—the theme of love and thoughts of the beloved, which never
left the poet in all his wanderings about Europe—the rejected conclusion had conjoined another theme: return and reunion. In the
fuller version, this elegy contained two clearly-defined, independent
parts. Therefore, in order to safeguard the unity of impression,
Batyushkov decided to sacrifice the second part. More than anything he wanted his poetry to convey to the readers a picture not
only of the poet, but also of the man:

> *I zhil tak tochno, kak pisal . . .* [18]
>
> And lived exactly as he wrote . . .

Batyushkov made the same requirements of his own *Collection*
as those which are implicit in his articles on other poets in the first

volume of *Essays*. He wanted, through his verses, to elucidate his own personality, his character, and his fate as a human being.

The tried device of putting together a collection of elegies to form something in the nature of a lyrical novel had already been practiced by Parny who, in later publications of his collection of elegies, replaced the various names of the objects of his adoration by one name, Eléonore, and by this alone gave a novelistic finish to all four books of elegies which make up his *Poésies érotiques*. To what an extent Parny himself considered the unity thus obtained an important achievement is evident from his speech on the occasion of his acceptance to the French Academy in which he severely criticizes Tibullus for not making Delia "the only inspiration of his songs."[19] Batyushkov could not follow either Tibullus or Parny, as in his original elegies the heroines usually remain unnamed; he retains the names in the translations, or often uses some stylized, poetic name. Thus, in his adaptation of Parny's elegies *The Ghost (Prividenie)* and *False Alarm (Lozhny strakh)* he put in the name of Chloe, not mentioned in the original, and, in *The Last Spring,* Delia.

The name of the heroine, therefore, could not have had any compositional significance for Batyushkov. Unity of mood was the aim which he set himself as he selected verses for the second volume of *Essays,* but a unity which should be conveyed through *variety,* through the whole thematic wealth of the elegiac répertoire. Batyushkov found room in *Essays* for elegies on the most different subjects from *Hope* and *To a Friend,* condensed dramas of ideas, to his *Bacchante* and *False Alarm,* which are dominated by triumphant sensuality. Between these two poles are elegies devoted to different stages in the experience of love, friendship, and on the fate of the poet. They are all characterized by the commingling of opposite feelings, in that each is far richer in content than appears on first reading.

So, in the elegy *My Genius (Moy geniy)*, the contrast between two types of human memory—"the memory of the heart" (*pamyat' serdtsa*) and "the memory of the mind" (*pamyat' rassudka*), is given in the first two lines:

> *O pamyat' serdtsa! Ty sil'ney*
> *Rassudka pamyati pechal'noy*[20]

> Remembrance of the heart! More power
> Have you than reason's sad remembrance.

Further on, in lines 3–15, the "remembrance of the heart" is shown as the keeper of the image of the beloved, of that good "genius" [or, as translated here, "guardian spirit"] which illumines and beautifies the life of the poet, sleeping and waking:

> And in a distant land and far
> You charm me with a honeyed semblance.
> I mind the voice of well-loved words,
> I mind the eyes of tender blue
> I mind the hair, the golden hue
> Of lightly, loosely dangling curls.
> Each detail of the simple dress
> I mind, and fond remembrance yet
> Recalls my peerless shepherdess.
> Dear image I cannot forget,
> My guardian spirit that does follow
> My wanderings through all separation!
> If I should sleep? Then to my pillow
> She'll stoop, sad sleep's sweet reparation.[21]

The theme of sadness, which at the beginning was called the content of memory, reappears in the last line and permits a brief glimpse into the abyss of the heart where the feeling of sadness, evidently hiding in its depth the memory of unrequited love, has its dwelling. Its presence and effect is felt in the tones employed to paint the picture of the beloved.

This elegy, like the others, uncovers the inner contradictions in man's emotional life, the simultaneous presence of different feelings and of contradictory attitudes in the same person toward himself, toward his own emotional condition, and toward the conflicts going on in his own soul. All this goes to make up that unity of content in the *Essays* which Batyushkov wished to express through a variety of themes and motifs.

> And the proud mind will not subdue
> Love—by cold, calculating words.[22]

So ends the elegy *Awakening* (*Probuzhdenie*). Not only here, but in almost all the elegies in this collection there is some reflection of the struggle between feeling and mind, heart and reason, love and sobering experience.

The life of the heart has its own laws; it does not correspond to the conditions in which man is placed by fate. Individual fate is made up of the intersections of the main roads of history and personal passions, those points which do not correspond in their directions. Such non-correspondence acquires a peculiarly tragic character in the fate of the poet.

Both in the elegy *Hesiod and Homer—Rivals* and in *The Dying Tasso,* Batyushkov had expressed his profound conviction that the fate of the poet cannot be other than unhappy, because society does not understand him and cannot share either his sympathies or his aspirations. Of Homer he writes:

> An orphan born in Samos, raised in pauperism,
> Attentive as a son, through Hellas lead the blind
> Old man, but nowhere could the two asylum find . . .
> Where is it to be found for talent, poverty?[23]

The last line is not in Millevoye at all, it was added by Batyushkov.

The fate of the poet, the contradictoriness of the emotional world of man, the incompatibility of moral values with the laws of history—all this complex of Batyushkov's ideas on contemporary man is present in *Essays.* But not everything had been said fully enough in his verses; much he had only been able to hint at, and therefore it was left to the next generation of poets, particularly to Pushkin and Baratynsky, to work out the implications of Batyushkov in all their fullness and complexity.

## IV   *The Search for New Ways*

The majority of readers and critics of *Essays* continued to live with the old notion that Batyushkov was the poet of carefree delight. Alexander F. Voeykov was not the only one to feel as he did when, in 1819, he wrote:

> . . . Your entrancing power
> Conjures love, wine and song, Fame's fevered hour.
> Horace and Muses' love, sweet-tongued Ovidius Naso,

> Anacreon and you, you honor yet the Graces
> And they, pure maids, come down to Neva's granite banks
> And 'neath the shady limes give you fair words and thanks
> While, in their company, on ice the blown rose blushes
> And iron-fingered frost daren't reach to pluck it.
> And the bright winter sun from cloudless skies invites
> To forests sylvan-cool and indolent delights.[24]

Batyushkov himself wrote to Gnedich: "Now, rereading the book, I see all its imperfections."[25] He had informed Zhukovsky some time before: "If God permits a second edition, I shall revise everything; maybe I shall write something new."[26]

A copy of *Essays* with corrections Batyushkov made between 1819 and 1821 has been preserved. Ten poems are crossed out in the list of contents of the second volume, mostly from the early verses and changes made in the texts of the others.

Alterations and emendations of old verses could not remain Batyushkov's chief creative preoccupation. He now had to define for himself what new thing he could write, what road he should now choose. When *Essays* was being printed and after it was published, Batyushkov's new literary plans were concentrated in two directions. He now mulled over plans for new verses—such as that for *Ovid in Scythia* ("a happier subject for an elegy than Tasso himself")[27] and worked on schemes for long poems.

His interest in the genre of the narrative poem was tied up with the new relationship into which he had entered with the young writers who had created the society of "Arzamas" in 1815. "Arzamas" had originally been formed as a private joke, for the drawing-room ridiculing of Admiral Shishkov's followers, and as Zhukovsky at that time had become the chief victim of their attacks, the members of "Arzamas" began taking the names of characters from his ballads. Zhukovsky himself was called Svetlana, Vyazemsky—Asmodeus, Bludov—Cassandra. Batyushkov, elected in his absence in 1815, was given the name of Achilles. The minutes of "Arzamas" show that there was always a division of opinion among the members. Some wished to give the Society a more serious and purposeful character and to publish a journal.[28] Batyushkov, who only began to attend the meetings of "Arzamas" in the second half of 1817, was in favor of the idea for a journal.

In 1817, illustrating Sergey Uvarov's article "On the Greek Anthology," Batyushkov translated twelve poems by ancient Greek poets. However, the dream of producing a journal came to nothing, and Batyushkov's translations, together with Uvarov's article, were not published until 1820.

In the circle of "Arzamas" the conversation often turned to how desirable and well-timed would be the creation of a long poem on a national, historical subject. From 1815 on, Batyushkov had been trying to persuade Zhukovsky to undertake a poem along these lines.[29] He also advised the young Pushkin to attempt the genre. Zhukovsky did plan to write a poem based on the ancient Russian epic of Prince Vladimir, but it never got beyond the stage of plans. From Batyushkov's letters we can see that he, too, had several epic Poems in mind. One of them was to have been entitled *Ryurik,* and he complained to Gnedich of the difficulties he had:

I was thinking of getting down to work on a *long poem.* It's been in my head for a good while. Like a hen, I am looking for a place to lay my egg, but can I find it, do you think? It seems I am doomed to die pregnant with my Ryurik. For him I need health, I need books, I need geographical maps, I need information, I need, I need, I need . . . and more talent than you happen to have, you will add. It is all quite true, yet it sits in my head and my heart, and make no effort to push forth: it is a torment.[30]

Plans for another poem were given in this same letter to Gnedich, with a request to send him: ". . . the Slavonic legends of Novikov. *Ancient Russian Verses* edited by Klyucharov, if I am not mistaken. Add to these *Bova-the-Prince, Pyotr of the Golden Keys, Ivashka-White Shirt,* and all that trash. With luck, I may some day get down to that as well."[31]

Having renounced his intention of writing the historical poem *Ryurik,* Batyushkov conceived the idea of another poem, the detailed plan of which he expounded in a letter to Vyazemsky. From this plan it is clear that it should have been something in the nature of a fairy tale with materials drawn from Russian folklore. The *dramatis personae* were to have been wizards *(volkhvy)* and water-sprites, and the hero was to find himself at the bottom of the Dnieper in the realm of the water-sprite Gada. However, all of Batyushkov's attempts at long poems came to nothing. He continued to write what, in the letter to Gnedich, he had called "trifles," that is, the shortest of short poems: "As to these trifles, I myself am heartily sick of them, but ill health confines me to such trifles."[32]

Many and various were the reasons why neither Zhukovsky nor Batyushkov wrote narrative poems, although both thought very seriously of this poetic genre. The venerable writer Karamzin added his voice to those of the young "Arzamas" writers in the hope that Batyushkov would write a great work. He wrote to him:

Write, whether in prose, or verse, only with feeling: everything will be fresh and powerful . . . and the result will be a charming child and a laurel wreath for the parent: a poem, such as Holy Russia has never seen before! Write me a portrait of Batyushkov, so that I may see him as in a mirror with all those fine traits natural to his heart, in the whole, not in fragments, so that future generations may come to know you as I know you, and to love you as I love you.[33]

Karamzin's concept of the narrative poem is very characteristic of those contradictory views of this genre prevailing in the literary circles closest to Batyushkov. Some considered that a narrative poem could be the result of a "composition"—a combination of elegiac themes—such as those which Batyushkov had already perfected with such brilliance. The trend of Russian literature toward the long, narrative poem, at last realized by Alexander Pushkin near the end of the 1810's showed that the genre could not be only an expression of the poet's personality; the narrative poem is not an extended version of the elegy, but a distinct literary form in which the author's poetical personality can exist only with the support of some outside material, whether taken from history, folklore, or ethnography. Batyushkov could not overcome his disdainful attitude to the literary, fairy tale folksiness which Pushkin borrowed from eighteenth-century sources and unhesitatingly transfigured to suit his own literary personality.

It would be wrong to take Batyushkov's words about "trifles" too literally. He was, after all, writing to Gnedich, a supporter of lofty themes and grand genre, and this explains the deprecating tone in which he writes of his own verses. The bitterness and irritation which can be detected in Batyushkov's words go to prove something quite different: the poet's dissatisfaction with all he had so far achieved and an acute awareness of the necessity of changing his manner, his themes, the whole structure of his lyric verse. And so, parallel with his consideration of subjects for large works, Batyushkov worked on lesser poetic forms in his translations for his *Greek Anthology* and then on his original cycle, *Imitations of the Ancients* (*Podrazhaniya drevnim*).

These lesser poetic forms might be described as "abbreviations" of Batyushkov's own elegies to a minimal size, in several cases to a single quatrain. Batyushkov threw out the descriptive motifs of his elegies, rejected the comparisons of past and present which form the basis of the elegiac subject, and retained only the elegiac situation, or rather a distillation of elegiac content.

Later, critics came to consider these "anthological"* verses of Batyushkov's his highest achievement. Belinsky thought them "the best product of his muse."[34]

His translation-adaptations from the anthology (not knowing Greek, Batyushkov used the French versions of Sergey Uvarov) are even more striking than the elegies in their concrete realism and in the precision of the situation:

> *Svershilos': Nikagor i plamenny Erot*
> *Za chashey Vakhovoy Aglayu pobedili . . .*
> *O, radost'! Zdes' oni sey poyas razreshili,*
> *Stydlivosti devicheskoy oplot,*
> *Vy vidite: krugom rasseyany nebrezhno*
> *Odezhdy pyshnye nadmennoy krasoty;*
> *Pokrovy lëgkie iz dymki belosnezhnoy,*
> *I obuv' stroynaya, i svezhie tsvety:*
> *Zdes' vse—razvaliny roskoshnogo ubora,*
> *Svideteli lyubvi i schast'ya Nikagora!*[35]

> At last! Hot Eros and enamored Nikagor
> With Bacchus' heady aid Aglaia here have vanquished . . .
> Oh, joy! On this same spot her virgin belt they ravished,
> And watched her maiden robes slip to the floor.
> See there: how carelessly lies scattered the brave show

---

* In Russian, this term is used for verses reminiscent (in style or content) of the lyrics of the Ancients as represented in their "Anthologies." According to the critic Belinsky, such lyrics are distinguished by "simplicity, unity of thought capable of expression in a small space, directness and loftiness of tone, plasticity and grace of form."

> Of haughty beauty's festive garments strewn;
> Light veils diaphanous as smoke and white as snow,
> And garlands of fresh flowers, and slender shoe.
> Here all about—the wreck of the bright garb she wore
> Bears witness to the love and luck of Nikagor.

After the first two lines, which take us immediately into the situation, there follows, without any preliminary explanations or introductions, the descriptive part of the verse. The object of this description is neither the persons about whom the poem is written, nor their emotional state, nor yet their actions. The picture of the triumph of love is conveyed through inanimate objects. It is not people, their feelings, or their actions which Batyushkov renders eloquent, but things.

This language of things, this deanimation and objectivization of psychological states is the most important feature of Batyushkov's poetic manner in his post-*Essays* work.

In another poem, this replacement of people by inanimate objects is shown as follows:

> *Svideteli lyubvi i goresti moey,*
> *O rozy yunye, slezami omochenny!*
> *Krasuytesya v venkakh nad khizhinoy smirennoy,*
> *Gde milaya taitsya ot ochey!*
> *Pomedlite, venki! eschchë ne uvyadayte!*
> *No esli yavitsya,—proleyte na neë*
> *Vsë blagovonie svoë*
> *I lokony eë slezami napitayte . . .*[36]

> You who have seen my love and heard my bitter sighs,
> Young climbing roses with fresh tears forever welling!
> Entwine with liveliness the unpretentious dwelling
> Where my beloved hides from prying eyes!
> Bloom on, you twining wreaths! Fade not yet from her bower!
> But should she show herself—then from your branches bent
> Engulf her in your balmy scent
> And shake down all your tears her curling locks to shower.

The roses are intended to convey the emotion; they can well replace man and his emotions, and can condense the power of his passion. The roses in this poem are very different from those roses of which Batyushkov wrote in the elegy *To a Friend*. There they were a poetic symbol, soaring far beyond the objective meaning and material essence of roses. In his translations *From a Greek Anthology* Batyushkov gave back the rose its nature; it again became a flower with a "balmy scent," a flower that could bloom and fade. In this poem the rose returns to its appointed place in man's environment.

Thus Batyushkov, in his anthological verses, worked out a new non-elegiac style perfectly suited to narrative genres and, therefore, to the long poem, the object of which would be the acts and deeds of men with inanimate objects occupying a subordinate position.

## V   *People and Things in the Anthological Verses*

In Batyushkov's anthological cycle, objects, by virtue of their newly recovered fullness of material being, their "thingness," acquire a completely new function (new in poetry): they can stand independent of a human character and take upon themselves the expression of psychological situations. An example of such a transition from the world of emotions to the world of things is contained in the following poem:

> *Iznemogaet zhizn' v grudi moey ostyloy.*
> *Konets boreniyu; uvy! vsemu konets.*
> *Kiprida i Erot, muchiteli serdets!*
> *Uslysh'te golos moy posledniy i unyly.*
> *Ya vyanu i eshchë mucheniya terplyu:*
> *Polmërtvy, no sgorayu;*
> *Ya vyanu, no eshchë tak plamenno lyublyu*
> *I bez nadezhdy umirayu!*
> *Tak, zhertvu obkhvativ krugom,*
> *Na altare ogon' bledneet, umiraet*
> *I, vspykhnuv yarche pred kontsom,*
> *Na peple pogasaet.*[37]

The end of pain and strife: alas, of all—the end.
Come Eros, Aphrodite! Hear me! I commend
To you, my torturers, my last-voiced lamentation.
I wither, and yet still I suffer agony.
Half-dead, yet burning I . . .

I wither, and yet still I move most ardently
And, void of every hope, I die!
E'en so the fire consumes the gift
Upon the altar, then, before the end, leaps higher,
One flame from graying embers left,
In ashes to expire.

In the concluding four lines this transition from the world of
emotions to the world of things is affected by the unfolding of a
detailed simile.

The fire of passion, the metaphorical fire consuming the subject
of the poem as he "dies" of love, is compared to a real, material,
natural fire. This brings about something in the nature of a realiza-
tion of the metaphor which, according to the canons of elegiac style,
is categorically forbidden.[38]

Everything which, in these final four lines, is represented as real
action, as the process of the incineration of the sacrifice by a perfectly real fire, is used in a periphrastic manner in the first eight lines
as the poet simultaneously develops two parallel themes—the
theme of death, the end, and the theme of the torments of unrequited passion.

The poem, as we see clearly from the invocation in the third line,
is a man's last pronouncement, his last prayer to the gods from
whom he waits in vain for help since it is they who are guilty of his
torments and his approaching death.

The second quatrain introduces a new theme—the theme of
fiery passion, unquenchable even by the imminence of the hero's
death. This new theme is introduced in the first line of the second
quatrain. In the following line, in contrast to the general state of
*dying,* the theme of *burning* "in the flames of passion" is introduced, while in the third and fourth lines the theme of death
and the theme of love are reconciled.

The poem is completed by an image-simile of real, not metaphorical fire, in the process of destroying its sacrificial victim.

Between the beginning and the end of the poem there is a peculiar thematic symmetry. In the first and twelfth (last) lines we
have the same motif of the dying fire, only expressed differently.
The theme of the end (death) first appears in the second line and
and surges up again in the (penultimate) eleventh. This, however,

is not a repetition of the same motif. The *end* in the context of
the first line is a synonym for *death* as the end of life, whereas
the second time the *end* has a direct, materially definable meaning, quite unmetaphorical.

The translations *From a Greek Anthology* were printed and
met with an enthusiastic reception by the young critics. Wilhelm
Küchelbecker, at that time the reviewer for the journal *Son of
the Fatherland* (*Syn Otechestva*)[39] quoted the end of the poem,
*Alas! That eyes of lustre dimmed by tears . . .*(*Uvy! glaza, potukhshie
v slezakh . . .* ), in which the poet writes of the possible "resurrection" of the lover if only his beloved will incline more favorably
toward him:

> *No ty, prelestnaya, kotoroy mne lyubov'*
> *Vsego—i yunosti i schastiya dorozhe,*
> *Sklonis', zhestokaya, i ya . . . voskresnu vnov'*
> *Kak byl ili eshchë bodree i molozhe.*[40]

> But you, enchantress, you whose love has proved my bane,
> Dearer to me than all, than youth or joy or wealth,
> Be gracious, cruel love, and I . . . shall rise again
> Just as I was, or younger—and in better health.

The critic gave the following appreciation of the mood and significance of this poem: "It is impregnated with that profound feeling which characterizes the modern elegy united with that robust-
ness, that fullness, which is the guiding principle of even the saddest
works of the Greeks."[41]

Küchelbecker perceived in Batyushkov's anthological verses
the poet's interest in depicting critical psychological situations,
typical of Batyushkov's work as a whole, and he commended the
absence of monotony.

This quality of Batyushkov's poetry was even more strikingly
expressed in the cycle *Imitations of the Ancients* (*Podrazhaniya
drevnim*), unpublished during the poet's lifetime and, for many
years, known only to a small circle of his friends. Batyushkov, however, on the off-chance of a second edition of his *Essays,* prepared
these poems for inclusion in the second part.

In this cycle Batyushkov varies his new outlook on inanimate
objects which, as concrete things, not metaphorical, are capable
of expressing emotions and psychological states and applies it to

themes taken from the most varied cultural and stylistic spheres, as, for example, the "Eastern" Style:

> *Skaly chuvstvitel'ny k svireli;*
> *Verblyud prislushivat' umeet pesn' lyubvi,*
> *Stenya pod bremenem; rumyanee krovi*
>  *Ty vidish'—rozy pokrasneli*
> *V doline Yemena ot pesney solov'ya . . .*
> *A ty, krasavitsa . . . Ne postigayu ya.*[42]

Tall cliffs incline to piping rushes;
The camel lends an ear to songs of love,
Groaning beneath his load; more red than blood
  See there—the rich rose blushes
In Yemen's vale to hear the nightingales . . .
But you, my Beauty . . . My comprehension fails

Love expressed by art (the reed pipe and the songs of love) or by nature (the nightingale's song) is able to enthrall everything in the world, everything in humanity. The indifference and coldness of the "Beauty" are not even mentioned; the degree of her unconcern and heartlessness can be judged only by contrast with the picture of the universal triumph of love over people, flowers, animals, even cliffs, that is, even over inanimate nature.

Nature inspired and permeated by passion is contrasted with a heartless human being, the soulless "Beauty." Things, objects, and inanimate nature all come to life in the poetry of Batyushkov while retaining their material phenomenality. Batyushkov's new style does not devour objects nor dematerialize the world; rather it infuses the objects themselves with spirit, imparting to them the emotional attributes of man. The feeling for history expressed in his elegies through the elegiac hero's views toward changes in individual human fates are now reproduced through the fate of things and man-made works:

> *Ty probuzhdaesh' sya, o Bayya, iz grobnitsy*
> *Pri poyavlenii Avrorinykh luchey,*
> *No ne otdast tebe bagryanaya dennitsa*
> *Siyaniya protekshikh dney,*
> *Ne vozvratit ubezhishchey prokhlady,*
> *Gde nezhilis' roi krasot,*

*I nikogda tvoi porfirny kolonnady*
*So dna ne vstanut sinikh vod.*[43]

From your deep sepulchre, oh Baiae, you awaken
At the first showing of Aurora's crimson rays,
But the bright sun will not restore what time has taken,
The splendor of your bygone days.
Will not restore those pleasant refuges of shade
Where thronged your once voluptuous daughters,
And never more will your porphyry colonnades
Rise from the blue depths of the waters.

All the emotional content of this verse is concentrated in the last
two lines. The "porphyry colonnades" buried beneath the waters
speak of the passing of time, of the irreversibility of the process,
of the destruction of a once magnificent and beautiful civiliza-
tion—the Roman Empire.

Material monuments of this past greatness, the porphyry
colonnades have remained, and the rarity and beauty of the stone
serve to emphasize the distinction of the art and the sheer wealth
of this irretrievably vanished age of man's history.

Batyushkov's anthological verses, not only those called *From
a Greek Anthology* and *Imitations of the Ancients*, but several
others as well, were unanimously admired by all later Russian
critics. Belinsky, as early as 1840, called these verses "the best
product of his muse," "truly exemplary, true artistry."[44] Of Batyushkov's anthological verses Belinsky wrote: "In his verse there is a
great plasticity, a great *sculptural* talent, if I may so put it. His verse
is often not only audible to the mind, but visible to the eye: one
feels an urge to run one's fingers over the curves and folds of the
drapery."[45] Belinsky himself, as is quite evident, used the term
sculptural in a figurative, not literal sense. He had in mind the
real treatment of material phenomena and poetization of the
world of things, which is particularly characteristic of Batyushkov's anthological verse. A literal interpretation of the term
"sculptural," impossible for Belinsky, gained currency among
some of his followers. This engendered the appearance of such
paradoxical and essentially senseless remarks as that passed by
A. D. Galakhov with respect to Batyushkov's poetry: "In his
works whole pieces were moulded like clearly defined *sculptures*
of thought and feeling."[46]

Belinsky's remark of the artistry of Batyushkov's anthological verses is interesting in that it corresponds to his general appreciation of Pushkin's poetry. By artistry Belinsky understood the peculiar power of poetry to give immediate expression to the aesthetic ideal to embody a harmonious image of a beautiful human being. Before Pushkin, only Batyushkov had achieved such artistry in all its fullness and power.[47]

## VI  *Batyushkov's School*

After *Essays,* in spite of the book's success with critic and reader, the poet entered upon a period of acute dissatisfaction with his position in life and literature, a period during which he devoted a great deal of energy to persistent efforts in obtaining a post at one of the Russian missions in Italy. After considerable delays, vexations, and wirepulling he achieved this ambition and, in 1819, arrived in Rome via Warsaw and Vienna. From Rome he proceeded to Naples in February to take up his duties there. Upon the recommendation of Alexey Olenin, Batyushkov made the acquaintance of a number of young Russian artists with whom he struck up friendly relations and with one of whom, the landscape painter S. F. Shchedrin, established himself in a flat in Naples.

At the beginning Batyushkov was enchanted by Naples and Pompeii. Naples and its surroundings supplemented his longstanding impressions gained from books with new content: "All around are picturesque views, the sea and, everywhere, associations with the past; here it is possible to read Pliny, Tacitus, and Virgil and put the muse of history and poetry to the proof of touch."[48] However, complaints of boredom and the lack of congenial society soon began to appear in his letters.

The Kingdom of Naples [actually, Kingdom of the Two Sicilies] was then governed by a reactionary government which cruelly suppressed any attempts at freethinking. Batyushkov, although he did not subscribe to the more extreme political views of Russian lovers of freedom and participants in secret revolutionary societies, was disgusted by the stagnancy and stuffiness of the social atmosphere in the Italian Kingdom: "It is very, very difficult to find a man you can so much as exchange views with. From Europe we are separated by seas and a Chinese wall. Madame de Staël was quite right when she said that Europe ends at Terracina."[49] At the same time, what depressed Batyushkov more than anything was that he had almost ceased to write poetry. Added to this, his relationships with the head of the Russian mission in Naples became extremely strained, and his work began to be a burden to him.

In 1820 a revolution broke out in Naples. This scared Batyushkov, a supporter of gradual reform and enlightenment. After he had left Naples for Rome in 1821, he wrote with irritability to his friends in Russia: "I am thoroughly fed up with this stupid revolution. It is time to be wise, that is, calm and still."[50]

In that same year, Batyushkov obtained leave from the Mission and left Italy in a more seriously disturbed psychological state than ever. The following year his depression developed into a serious psychic illness. Attempts were made to cure him; he was treated at a psychiatric home in Saxony, then placed under the care of his sister in Moscow, after which, from 1833 to his death, he lived with his nephew, G. A. Grevens, in Vologda.

Sometimes he had periods of lucidity. To Vyazemsky, who happened to visit him in one such moment, he said: "What is there to be said about my verses!... I am like a man who did not reach his goal, but was carrying a beautiful vessel on his head, with something in it. The vessel slipped from his head, fell, and was shattered to pieces. Just try to reestablish now what was in it!"[51]

While Batyushkov was opening up new poetic vistas and making important alterations in his style, working out a new feeling for things for himself and for Russian poetry in general, his former achievements, and particularly his elegiac manner, were being rapidly and increasingly adapted in Russian literature. A very significant number of young poets was occupied in developing Batyushkov's elegiac style. Thus, Evgeny Baratynsky constructed his *Epistle to Baron Delvig* (*Poslanie k baronu Delvigu*) as a combination of motifs from Batyushkov's elegy *To a Friend* and his verse letter *My Penates*. Baratynsky's poem has its own feeling for life, which differs in quality from the doubts to which Batyushkov gives voice in his elegy, but the stylistic similarity is indisputable.

Baratynsky's *Country Elegy* is also an independent variation on themes from the *Elegies from Tibullus*. Having learned to exploit Batyushkov's elegiac style for his own purposes, Baratynsky was not slow in overcoming the influence of his teacher, and in 1821–22 was already altering the elegy's internal structure. "His interest," a modern scholar justly remarks, "was now engaged not as much by the general lyrical evocation of any one elegiac senti-ment—melancholy, sadness, joy, love, disenchantment—but with those various, everchanging, and occasionally extremely con-tradictory shades of feeling which they acquire in their specifically psychological manifestations. In this way the lyrical theme which Batyushkov works out straightforwardly on a single emotional plane acquires inner movement and psychological penetration in the early works of Baratynsky."[52]

Baratynsky was, however, the only young Russian poet of the early 1820's who dared to adopt such an independent attitude to-wards Batyushkov's poetry. The others, with the exception, of course, of Alexander Pushkin, could not free themselves from Batyushkov's compelling influence, and continued to write varia-tions on his elegiac themes and images. The early work of the young Kondrati Ryleev, for instance, who later became the poet of civic themes, is simply made up of echoes from Batyushkov's elegies.[53]

Toward the mid-1820's the attitude toward poetry in Russian literature began to change. The elegy, not so much as a genre but as a trend, "the dismal elegy," became the object of bitter critical polemics.[54] Not only Batyushkov's imitators, but he himself, together with Zhukovsky, were condemned by the advocates of that branch of Russian Romanticism which demanded that poetry oc-cupy itself with national, historical themes, and primarily with heroic and civic subjects.

In 1823 O. Somov wrote in a long tract *On Romantic Poetry* (*O romanticheskoy poezii*): "All kinds of poetry have now al-most flowed together into the one elegiac mode: everywhere we have dismal dreams, the desire for we-know-not-what, world-weariness, the longing for something better, expressed incomprehensibly and filled with ill-chosen words, pirated from one or another of our most popular poets."[55] If Batyushkov is not actually named here, he is without a doubt included. Finally, in the following year, Wilhelm Küchelbecker, who but a few years before had wel-comed the appearance of *Essays in Verse and Prose* and *From a Greek Anthology,* now declared the elegies of Batyushkov, to-gether with the elegies of Zhukovsky and Pushkin, to be an out-of-date genre, powerless to express new, historically progressive, social content: "Once you have read one elegy . . . you know the lot. We have long been empty of feeling: the feeling of melancholy has swallowed up all the rest. We all seek to outdo one another in yearning over our lost youth; endlessly we chew the cud of this yearning and compete in airing our pusillanimity in periodical publications."[56] Further, he goes so far as to call Batyushkov an imitator and not an original poet: "he took as his model two pigmies of French literature: Parny and Millevoye."[57]

The war against the "dismal" elegy, against the elegiac trend in poetry in the mid-1820's, bears witness to the fact that direct reproductions of elegiac themes and images from Zhukovsky's and Batyushkov's poetry no longer satisfied the literary requirements of the rising generation. The elegy was now required to individualize feelings and situations in a way that Batyushkov's poetry did not. Batyushkov's elegiac style began to be felt as a distinctive poetical form from which all content had long since evaporated.

Essentially this was unjust, but the development of literature was proceeding as it had to, according to its own inflexible laws. What had seemed and indeed *was* a real artistic discovery in Batyushkov's elegies at the time of the publication of *Essays* in 1817, was already felt to be an empty repetition of meaningless, poetic formulae in 1824. Everything fruitful in Batyushkov's elegies had been organically assimilated by Pushkin and Baratynsky, and that is why it was Batyushkov's anthological, not his elegiac verses which lived on and continued to influence the development of Russian poetry. These anthological verses of Batyushkov's, as it happened, were destined to lead a long, independent existence throughout the Pushkin period and, perhaps it would not be too much to say, right up to the present day.

## VI   *Pushkin and Batyushkov*

The literary relationship between Batyushkov and Pushkin was a complex, two-sided process. To begin with, Batyushkov was Pushkin's model and teacher; however, as early as 1815, Pushkin was looking for his own way, though in his elegies of 1816–1817 this quest for poetic independence went no further than the free combination of motifs from the poetry of Zhukovsky and Batyushkov.

At the end of 1816 and the beginning of 1817, Pushkin, follow-ing the examples of Zhukovsky and Batyushkov, was already think-ing of publishing a collection of his verses. With the help of his lycée friends, he copied them into an exercise book entitled *The Verses of Alexander Pushkin, 1817*. At the same time he gave Zhukovsky a plan for a future collection in which the basic sections, as in Batyushkov's *Essays,* were to be "Elegies" and "Epistles."[58] The elegiac cycle of 1816 is also founded on the motifs and style the younger poet had assimilated from the elegies of Zhukovsky and Batyushkov. Among those closest in spirit to Batyushkov is *Autumn Morning* (1816), in which a great deal in the lyrical situa-tion, the repeated motif of the disappearance of the beloved, and the style is reminiscent of Batyushkov's 1815 elegies.

Not only while he was at the Lycée, but even after he had com-pleted his education, Pushkin still remained under the influence of Batyushkov's elegies. For example, one elegy written in 1818, *Convalescence,* unites subject motifs from Batyushkov's elegy of the same name and from *My Penates*.[59]

However, the elegy was already occupying Pushkin less than dur-ing the lycée period. Of the *petits genres* he was now attracted to the epistolary, which he used as a kind of political poetry. Another object of his endeavor and thoughts between 1817 and 1820 was the narrative poem, on which, as we have already seen, both Batyushkov and Zhukovsky were fruitlessly engaged.

Epistolary verse is the genre in which Pushkin was working with particular intensity between 1817 and 1820, that is, at the same time he was writing his first long poem *Ruslan and Lyudmila*. Letters in verse are the freest conceivable genre, least circumscribed by rules and regulations of literary precedent.[60] Nevertheless, in spite of all the freedom which Pushkin felt in handling this genre, he had not completely overcome and reassimilated the heritage of Batyushkov, who had been the pioneer of this particular type of informal epistle in *My Penates*.

For this reason, Pushkin deliberately elaborated his own varia-tions on the theme of Batyushkov's epistle which was one of his favorites. The theme of death, very important in *My Penates,* which can be sensed between the lines throughout the poem, al-though it is spoken of directly only in the concluding lines—after the address to the poet's friends—sets the tone and content of

Pushkin's *To Krivtsov* (*Krivtsovu*, 1819) from the very outset:

> Do not scare us, dearest friend,
> That the the grave awaits us humans.
> Faith, we've better things to do than
> Contemplate our latter end.[61]

Those in whose name Pushkin replies to a common "friend" are skeptics and epicureans like the "friend" himself; the epistle is addressed to an intimate friend, to "one of us," to a fellow-spirit who has suddenly reminded his companions of the possibility and inevitability of death.

The situation in *My Penates* is reversed: in Batyushkov's poem the poet addresses his poet friends with a hymn to pagan epicureanism; in Pushkin's, the poet addresses one of his own circle of fellow-spirits in the name of all the rest.

Rejecting the slow and gradual approach of old age and, after it, death, Pushkin, like Batyushkov, considered only youth as life; and all its joys end when youth ends.[62] Pushkin, however, introduces a motif not to be found in Batyushkov—the motif of the poet's deliberate poetic organization of his own death.

The end of the epistle *To Krivtsov* is similar in meaning to the end of *My Penates;* both in Batyushkov's and Pushkin's poems not sorrow, but joy and beauty remain as a reminder of the fortunate young man who left this life still intoxicated with its joys, but without fear or regret. In this epistle the theme of overcoming the fear of death—the theme of the triumph of man as the artist of his own fate, subject to death and religion—stands in a complex relationship with Batyushkov's poetry as a whole. Pushkin does not only give his own version of the themes and images of *My Penates,* but, at the same time, advances his own poetic arguments against Batyushkov's elegy *To a Friend,* in which the theme of death and its triumph over man, over the fate of mankind in general, is developed more fully and with more artistic power than elsewhere.

"Pilgrims one minute's span, we walk on dead men's graves"—this is the poetic definition of life which Batyushkov offers in his elegy.

The opening lines of Pushkin's epistle sound like direct polemics with Batyushkov:

> Do not scare us, dearest friend
> That the grave awaits us humans . . .

Pushkin's epistles and his poem attracted the acute, intense interest of Batyushkov. He followed Pushkin's work on *Ruslan and Lyudmila*, enlisting the support of mutual friends urging them to hurry him along; he listened to readings of those cantos which were ready before he left for abroad. To Vyazemsky in Moscow, Batyushkov wrote that "young Pushkin is writing a delightful poem and maturing."[63] In the opinion of L. N. Maykov, Batyushkov, with his touchy professional pride, "must have felt that new artistic forces were coming into being before his very eyes. . . . It is, therefore, quite understandable that a shade of rivalry entered into the relationship between our poet and that lucid genius who . . . was merrily striking out on his own new road, even while he still acknowledged himself Batyushkov's pupil."[64] How jealously Batyushkov reacted to Pushkin's poetic innovations is recorded by one of his contemporaries: "There is a story going around how Batyushkov convulsively screwed up in his hands a piece of paper on which he had been reading *A Letter to Yuriev* and exclaimed before he could stop himself: 'Oh, how that villain can write!'"[65]

Thus with profoundly mixed feelings Batyushkov greeted the stream of new poetical masterpieces which flowed from Pushkin's pen and, it seems, continued to reach him as his mind sank deeper and deeper into a state of manic depression.

We know that Batyushkov was generous in praise of certain chapters of *Ruslan and Lyudmila,* and asked eagerly that this poem, so "full of beautiful things and promises," should be sent to him in Naples. However, it seems likely that he never received it, as at that time it was an extremely complicated business to procure books from Russia. Whenever it was that Batyushkov did read this poem, his feelings must have been akin to those of Zhukovsky who, after the publication of *Ruslan and Lyudmila,* inscribed a portrait of himself which he was presenting to Pushkin: "To the victor-pupil from the vanquished teacher."[66] Pushkin's successes and triumphs very much complicated Batyushkov's quest for new ways on which his thoughts had been fixed ever since the publication of *Essays.* It is possible that, without wishing to do so, Wilhelm Küchelbecker, the most serious and thoughtful critic of the early 1820's may have inflicted a painful wound to Batyushkov's self-esteem. In his review of the verses and prose in the brochure entitled *From a Greek Anthology,* Küchelbecker ventured the unexpected opinion apropos of the author of the anonymously published verses:

> We do not know which of our poets concealed his name behind these translations . . . but if we are to judge by the pleasure one receives from reading his verses, by the sweetness of the melody of each one of them and, particularly, by the remarkable art with which each poetic period is set and maintained, by the great perfection of the prosody, a perfection which remains unattainable for some of our best poets and of which only two are consummate masters: it must be we are indebted either to Batyushkov or to the young singer of Ruslan. We are in doubt which of the two we have to thank for this gift to Russian literature, the transplantation of these sweet-scented, beautiful Greek flowers into our Russian soil.[67]

Finally, however, Küchelbecker opts for the assumption that Batyushkov was the author. Thus, on the admittance of the most refined connoisseurs of poetry, Pushkin had by that time completely caught up with Batyushkov, had achieved an equal degree of artistic perfection.

According to B. V. Tomashevsky, the language of Pushkin's first long narrative poem is fundamentally based on that of his elegies, and through those on the elegies of Zhukovsky and Batyushkov. He quotes a very convincing example of the direct connection between the language of Pushkin and that of Batyushkov's elegies:

> Pushkin:
> *Trepeshcha, khladnoyu rukoy*
> *On voproshaet mrak nemoy.*[68]
>
> All trembling, with a freezing hand,
> Of the dumb darkness he inquired

Batyushkov, in the elegy *I Feel my Gift for Poetry Extinguished* (*Ya chuvstvuyu, moy dar v poezii pogas*):

> *Rukoyu trepetnoy on mraki voproshchaet . . .*[69]
> With trembling hand of the pitch-darkness he inquired.

This juxtaposition is significant insofar as it bears witness to the profound, inward commingling of the styles of Batyushkov and Zhukovsky in Pushkin's poetry, to their organic assimilation, and, it follows, to the perfect elaboration of their poetic achievements in the work of their pupil.

In Pushkin's anthological verses written between 1820–1821 and printed later in the cycle *Imitations of the Ancients,* he achieved a synthesis of the elements which most appealed to him in Batyushkov's *Imitations of the Ancients* and other anthological verses. His elegy *The Flying Bank of Clouds Is Flimsier Far* (*Redeet oblakov letuchaya gryada,* 1820) originally entitled *The Tavrida Star* (*Tavricheskaya Zvezda*) is, in fact, a reworking of the thematic motifs and style of Batyushkov's *Tavrida* elegy.

Batyushkov shows us his imaginary picture of the Black Sea scene as an artistic evocation of the world of anthological poetry:

> Beneath the honeyed heaven of a Southern land
> . . . . . . . . . . . . . . . . . . . . . . . . . . . . . . . . . .
>
> Where ash trees spread their shade o'er meadows murmurously
> Where herds of wild horses, charging thunderously,
> For sound of cooling streams which rush beneath the earth . . . [70]

Here there is a self-evident similarity between the beautiful landscape which Pushkin recalls in his elegy and this enchanting scene from *Tavrida:*

> And I recall, familiar orb, your rising
> Above that peaceful land, all joys comprising,
> Where slender poplar in the valley grows,
> Where tender myrtle and dark cypress doze,
> And languorously the Southern seas are breaking.[71]

Another one of Pushkin's anthological poems, one particularly dear to the author, *The Muse* (*Muza,* 1821), was compared when it first came out to Batyushkov's *The Bower of the Muses* (*Besedka muz*). In Batyushkov's poem, the poet, in the middle of his life and poetry, dreams of a return to that state of heart and mind which is only natural to youth:

> He begs the Muses to redeem his soul from cares,
> To give him back the long-lost love of art,
> The unclouded merriment of those first, early years
> And feeling strong and fresh to his time-calloused heart.[72]

Pushkin, following Batyushkov, looks back to his poetical youth and reproduces in his poem the antique mythological idea of the first attempts, the first steps of a beginner in poetry. In Pushkin's poem as in Batyushkov's, there are no actual biographical hints. They are verses about the poet in general, about that state of peace occurring when poetic inspiration comes to a man naturally, out of his very nature, and not as a result of academic or bookish impressions.

Pushkin does not introduce into his anthological verses that dissonance with the ideal of which Batyushkov speaks in his *Bower of the Muses*—and that is the principal difference between them.

On the whole, Pushkin's anthological verses are a deliberate and conscious development of the principles in Batyushkov's post-1819 anthological verses, made more complex by his knowledge of André Chénier's poetry.

## VIII   *The Traditions of Batyushkov*

Russian anthological poetry, of which Batyushkov was the creator and initiator, continued to elaborate on his themes from the 1830's to the 1850's, varying his images, and enriching and modifying his anthological style of using concrete objects to convey the emotional and human.

Of course, Russian anthological poetry of the mid-nineteenth and early twentieth centuries owes its wealth and artistic perfection not to Batyushkov alone. Of no less importance than his anthological verses for the subsequent development of this particular poetical sphere in Russian literature was the poetry of Pushkin and Chénier. The latter, who was discovered only in 1819 by European critics, was assimilated by Russian poets between 1820 and 1840 both directly and through Pushkin's anthological cycles of the early 1820's, in which the fundamental, original feature of Chénier's poetry—his principle of expressing new, "contemporary" thoughts in antique form—was elaborated by applying them to Russian literary traditions.

This closeness to Batyushkov was something which Pushkin made no attempt to disguise and when he published his collection, *Verses* (*Stikhotvoreniya*, 1826), he—like Batyushkov—entitled one cycle *Imitations of the Ancients*. Tomashevsky was right when he pointed out that: "In fact, among the verses of this cycle, with the exception of the poem *Land and Sea* (*Zemlya i more*), there were no imitations in the literal sense of the word. However, in all these brief verses . . . there was that peculiar balance of poetic images, that peculiar plasticity of visual description, which, in the Age of Pushkin, were held to be the inherent qualities of antique poetry."[73]

It was the manner, inherited from Batyushkov, of suggesting an emotional state, emotional excitement through physical attitudes ("vzor potupleny" "down-cast gaze") and the frankness in the attitude toward love as a feeling in which passion is not enshrouded in romantic mists ("tvoy vzor . . . zhelaniem gorit" "your gaze . . . burns with desire"), but speaks out directly, totally obsessive, leaving no room for reflection, doubts, or hesitations. It was this strength, fullness, and wholeness of feeling which, according to Pushkin's understanding, was the distinguishing characteristic of the Ancients. The feelings which are treated in the poems of this cycle, and the forms in which these feelings are expressed, are not a direct translation as in Batyushkov—a direct reproduction of the subjects and imagery of the Greek anthology. Pushkin infinitely broadened the scope of anthological poetry, emancipating it from its roots deeply set in what was called a definite historic epoch—antiquity.

The post-Pushkin development of Russian anthological poetry in the 1840's and 1850's, in the works of Apollon Maykov, Afanasy Fet, and Nikolay Shcherbin combined the various tendencies originating both from Batyushkov and Pushkin.

Following Batyushkov, this poetry originally elaborated genuine antique themes and motifs, recreating the actual life of this world of beautiful human beings and beautiful art. Although following his general principles, unlike Batyushkov, they usually invoke the objective incarnation of this beautiful world in the guise of works of art and, more often than not, in works of sculpture. This reproduction—the recreation in words of plastic art works of antiquity—was one of the most characteristic phenomena in Russian anthological poetry of the mid-nineteenth century.

Afanasy Fet, then just at the beginning of his career, in his *Bacchante* (1840) repeated to a great extent Batyushkov's poem of the same title written in 1815. Like Batyushkov, Fet constructs the entire poem as an evocation of the orgiastic merriment and wild feelings of Bacchantes and Satyrs, carried away by mass emotion during the feast of Bacchus, the god of wine and merriment.

The resemblance between the two poems extends even to certain single expressions. A comparison is all the more interesting because of those developments in Russian anthological poetry which had taken place some time between the 1830's and the 1840's, and which can be traced by following the radically changing elaboration of the Bacchante theme.

In the collection, *The Verses of A. Maykov* (*Stikhotvoreniya A. Maykova,* 1842) the heroine of the poem *Bacchante* is shown in a quiet setting:

> At the dark grotto's mouth a young Bacchante lay
> At rest on one bare arm, her robes in disarray.
> ................................
> How troubled the wild vine upon her breathing breast,
> How ardently the lips, where smiles elusive play,
> Still move as if to speak their langour and their fire.[74]

The feeling experienced by the heroine of this poem is suggested purely statically. Nevertheless, the departure from the dynamic movement of Batyushkov's anthological verse by the poets of the 1840's did not indicate the complete renunciation of his traditions. In many ways they continued his work on anthological themes.

From Batyushkov they inherited and maintained the tendency to reproduce in words the beauty of the works of art of the Ancient World. But more than that, to Batyushkov, and not to Pushkin, should be traced the mid-century poets' desire to reproduce not only the material forms of antique sculptures, not only their texture, but to penetrate their inner content, to give a soul to marble, humanity to bronze, and to find in the statue a human being.

Such, for instance, is Fet's famous *Diana* (1850), the object of ardent enthusiasm among his contemporaries. Throughout the entire poem, the poet's passionate desire to see this beautiful creature in movement, to feel the life in it, is contrasted with the immobility and dispassion of the marble statue. The poem ends on an affirmation of the eternal stillness in which the goddess has her being.

Thus, the "Batyushkov principle"—Batyushkov's tradition of anthological poetry—is in Fet's verse, interwoven with Pushkin's tradition of anthological lyrics in which antique form usually carried contemporary content. This tendency, however, was of less significance in the poetry of the mid-nineteenth century.

Enthusiasm by Batyushkov for the perfection and harmony of the live human being of the Ancient world had been transmuted to an admiration for antique art which, for them, had become the ideal against which they measured life itself. As L. Lotman has pointed out: "It was not the closeness of art to reality which they felt as the source of beauty; rather, the degree to which Nature could be made to resemble art by a strict selection based on definite aesthetic canons was, for them, true beauty.[75]

A good illustration of this thought is Fet's second attempt at the Bacchante theme, this time realized in a very similar manner to that adopted by Maykov. In his 1843 *Bacchante,* Fet shows her standing still, having broken for a moment from her headlong circling in the whirl of the Bacchanalia; the living woman is shown as though she were a statue, marble come to life.

> The slender eyes, all moist with brimming tears,
> Sought slowly all about, full of bemused desire.[76]

Batyushkov's anthological themes and images continued to be reflected in Russian poetry of the early twentieth century, though to a lesser degree than in the mid-nineteenth century. The poets of the new century were more attracted by the possibility of showing contemporary conflicts and discovering new thoughts through antique themes and images. Such, for instance, are the anthological verse of Valery Bryusov in the cycle *Those Whom the Gods Love* (*Lyubimtsy bogov*) published in the collection *The Third Watch* (*Tretya strazha,* 1898–1901) and the cycle *The Eternal Truth of Idols* (*Pravda vechnaya kumirov*) in the collection *The Wreath* (*Venok,* 1904–1905). From myths and historical figures of antiquity, Bryusov seeks to reproduce those features which seem to him most significant in contemporary man: the intensity and depths of passion, the boldness of the challenge to Fate and to the Gods.

The Batyushkov principle was resurrected in the twentieth century in the poetry of Anna Akhmatova who continued that expression of feelings through things which we find in Batyushkov's

anthological verses. Akhmatova grasped Batyushkov's concrete
manner and plasticity through the almost century-old tradition of
Russian anthological poetry. Thus, in her verses an antique statue
may be seen as a contrast to the living, passionate, suffering human
being, as for example in her poem, *Love* (*Lyubov'*).

Batyushkov's poetry was also reflected in the work of Osip
Mandelshtam, who deliberately turned to his elegies and anthological images to express his own thoughts and experiences. The theme
of separation from the beloved, so insistently repeated in Batyushkov's verses on themes from Tibullus, is repeated again by Mandelshtam, including the "Delia" we remember from Batyushkov's
elegies, the peaceful country pursuits, details of domestic life, and
the theme of parting. It is as though Mandelshtam were deliberately
conjuring up the memory of his master, to whom he devoted a deeply
felt poem *Batyushkov* (1932)—a poem, which contains these
remarkable and intensely experienced words:

> With him he brought us our wealth and our anguish,
> Tongue-tied, the glorious burden he bears—
> Tumult of poetry, bell of true friendship,
> And a harmonious downpour of tears.[77]

The anthological tradition of Russian twentieth-century poetry
which clearly goes back to Batyushkov, has become a living fer-
ment in the literary process. The break with Symbolism, the reorien-
tation toward the material world of things took place in the 1910's
with a return to poetry of the Pushkin and pre-Pushkin era. Russian
twentieth-century poets remembered Batyushkov and found in his
works a still far from exhausted mine of poetic revelations, which
turned out to be needed and timely in their own artistic quests.

# Conclusion

IT was but briefly—a mere ten years—that Batyushkov, through his poetry, played a leading role in the development of Russian literature. And even this time was greatly reduced by wars and the trials and duties which attended them. As early as 1817, before the publication of *Essays in Verse and Prose,* Batyushkov wrote of this collection to Zhukovsky: "Why have I taken it into my head to print it? I feel, I know that much of it is worthless stuff, the very verses which cost me so much, now pain me. But could they have been better? What sort of life was I leading for verses? Three wars, all on horseback, and in peacetime without a home to call my own. I ask myself: was it possible to write anything perfect in so stormy, inconstant a life? Conscience answers: No!"[1] These words are indisputably exaggerated, but they are nevertheless typical of the attitude of this poet of "indolence" and "carelessness" to the main business of his life— his poetry. Also, while agreeing with him that the circumstances of his life were not conducive to creative work, we should, in any attempt to evaluate his overall achievement, allow ourselves to be swayed not so much by this *cri de coeur* of an exigent artist, as by the judgments of contemporary criticism.

In 1820, John Bowring, the compiler of an anthology of Russian poetry translated into English, included Batyushkov's *My Penates* together with verses by Lomonosov, Derzhavin, Zhukovsky, Karamzin, and Dmitriev.[2]

A modern scholar has made a detailed analysis of this translation and finds that, on the whole, it gives an accurate impression of the contents and, to some extent, of the style of the original.[3] For us, the interest shown by John Bowring in Batyushkov's poetry is one more confirmation of the fact that, after the publication of *Essays,* the importance of Batyushkov's poetry was no longer in question. Batyushkov was generally acknowledged as a poet of the new generation, of the new school. Bowring's anthology appeared chronologically midway between two typical contemporary comments. In 1817 Sergey Uvarov and, in 1823 Alexander Bestuzhev defined Batyushkov's place in the literature of their day in precisely the same way. Uvarov's opinion we have already quoted.[4] At the time of the publication of *Essays*, Uvarov was a very moderate liberal, whereas Bestuzhev, in 1823, was one of the most spirited members of the secret "Northern Society"—a convinced revolutionary; yet both had made similar comments in summing up the significance of Batyushkov's poetry. Bestuzhev wrote: "With Zhukovsky and Batyushkov there begins a new school in our poetry."[5]

In what lay the originality of this school?

The answer to this question may be given at different levels of research. Pushkin called it "the school of harmonious precision,"[6] because for him it was its stylistic characteristics that were important, its stylistic significance which he, as a recent adept, understood very well indeed. In her new work on Russian lyric poetry, L. Ya. Ginzburg gives a very sensitive and interesting delineation of the stylistic principles of Batyushkov in the chapter on "The School of Harmonious Precision."[7] Her interest lies mainly with the relationship of this school to the word in its actual stylistic functions: "The style of the Russian elegiac school is a most characteristic example of a firmly enclosed style, impenetrable for the raw, aesthetically unpolished everyday word. All the elements of this perfectly worked out system are subjected to one and the same goal—they are intended to express the beautiful world of a finely sensitive soul."[8]

In this definition, L. Ya. Ginzburg comes close to the conception of Batyushkov so well expounded by G. A. Gukovsky, who considers Zhukovsky and Batyushkov to be representatives of psychological Romanticism.[9] Gukovsky's point of view is challenged by N. V. Fridman and G. P. Makogonenko, who make a sweeping denial of any participation whatsoever on Batyushkov's part in the Romantic trend of literature.[10] Fridman considers him rather a pre-Romantic who failed to evolve to a full assimilation of Romantic aesthetic principles.[11]

The perfectly legitimate study of Batyushkov's poetry within the framework of the "school of harmonious precision" does not, however, do away with the questions either of his relationships to literary trends of the epoch or of his place in the general development of poetry.

It is possible to approach the solution to either of these questions taken separately or to both of them together from an angle which has hitherto proved least attractive to students of Batyushkov's style: with respect to the formula for a "school of harmonious precision" the first half—the problem of harmony, that is, the organization of sound within the verse—was of no less importance to Batyushkov than the problem of precision. In 1817, already looking back over his ten-year poetic activity and drawing conclusions, he wrote of Derzhavin's poems: "Every language has its own flow of words, its harmony, and it would be strange for a Russian, or an Italian, or an Englishman to write for the French ear, or the other way around. Harmony, bold harmony does not always depend on fluency. I know no verses which flow more fluently than these:

> *Na svetlogolubom efire*
> *Zlataya plavala luna . . .*

> Through pale blue ether smoothly sailing
> A golden moon was born aloft . . . .

in Derzhavin's *Ode to a Nightingale.* But what great harmony there is in the *Waterfall* or in the ode *On the Death of Meshchersky:*

> *Glagol vremën, metalla zvon!"*[12]
> Word of Ages, ring of metal!

From this judgment given by Batyushkov it is clear that he had a broad understanding of harmony in poetry as a complex system of an organization of sounds and did not reduce it to mere "fluency," that is, to the deliberate selection of words with liquid consonants, free of the "r" sound and of sibilants, the abundance of which in the Russian language had once seemed to him a serious obstacle on the way to the creation of a harmonious style. However, Batyushkov was persuaded by his own practice that it is possible to find harmonizing devices in any language that are suited to its phonetic nature, although, for him, Italian poetry always remained the ideal of poetic harmony.

Pushkin, in his notes along the margins of Batyushkov's *Essays,* carefully singled out examples of successful harmonization. Opposite two lines from the epistle *To a Friend,* he wrote: "Italian sounds! What a miracle-worker this Batyushkov!"[13]

He was referring to the lines:

*Nrav tikhiy angela, dar slova, tonkiy vkus,*
*Lyubvi i ochi i lanity.*[14]

Gentle, angelic temperament, eloquence, refined taste,
Eyes and cheeks made for love

Why was it that Pushkin should be so delighted by the "Italian" sounds in this poem of Batyushkov's? Surely there is no deliberate intention in the choice of liquid or sonorous consonants? Most probably Pushkin had in mind one of the pecularities of Italian poetry often used by Batyushkov's favorites Petrarch and Tasso, the so-called hiatus, caused by a conglomeration of vowels at the ends and beginnings of words, which was categorically forbidden by Boileau and condemned by Voltaire. In the second of the lines Pushkin marked, there is a hiatus which really does give it an "Italian" sound:

*Lyubvi i ochi.*

Such "Italian" conglomerations of vowels are met with frequently in Batyushkov's poetry. A few more examples are:

*Gromkiy voy ikh . . .*
Their loud howling
*No mne miley eë potuplennye vzory . . .*
But I prefer her lowered gaze
*Kiprida i Erot muchiteli serdets . . .*
Aphrodite and Eros, tormentors of men's hearts.

Of course, the deliberate use of the hiatus was by no means Batyushkov's only device for the harmonization of his verses; his technique and methods in this respect were extremely varied.[15]

Harmonization was so important a part of Batyushkov's style that it has been incorporated into the generally accepted definition on a level with precision. It would be of great service to the understanding of the essential quality of Batyushkov's poetry if the relationship between harmonization and his other creative principles could be established, particularly its relationship to the expression of the inward through the exterior, the emotional through the physical, through the dynamism of movement. Victor Vladimirovich Vinogradov has noted that in Batyushkov's poetry "Emotion and experience are depicted by means of subtle and varied descriptions of outward expressions and manifestations. For instance:

*Krasavitsa stoit, bezmolvstvuya, v slezakh,*
*Edva na zhenikha vzglyanut' ukradkoy smeet,*
*Potupya yasny vzor, krasneet i bledneet*
*Kak mesyats v nebesakh . . . "*[16]

The beauteous maid stands still, in silence and in tears,
She steals a glance toward her bridegroom and her courage nearly fails,
Her clear eyes are cast down, now flushed is she, now pale,
Like the moon in heaven.

Vinogradov goes on to develop this line of thought by pointing out that "Batyushkov was the first one before Pushkin to affirm the device of indirect expressive representation of feeling through naming the outward movements which accompany it, movements, moreover, at once intimate, profoundly personal and discreet, not eye-catching, but touching and affecting. For instance:

*Tam startsy zhadny slukh sklonyali k pesni sey,*
*Sosudy polnye v desnitsakh ikh drozhali,*
*I gordye serdtsa s vostorgom vspominali*
*O slave yunykh dney."*[17]

There old men hungrily give ear to the Scald's lays;
The brimming vessels in their right hands trembled,
And their proud hearts with eagerness remembered
The tales of their young days.

The Soviet scholar I. M. Semenko has studied the contrasting manners of Batyushkov and Zhukovsky. The conclusion she reached was similar: "Characteristic of Batyushkov is the depiction of feeling through its outward manifestations: 'Tvoya ruka v moey to mlela, to pylala' (*Mshchenie*) (Your hand in mine, now trembling limp, now fevered) (*Vengeance*); 'Edva na zhenikha vzglyanut' ukradkoy smeet . . . Krasneet i bledneet kak mesyats v nebesakh' (*Na ravalinakh zamka v Shvetsii*) (She steals a glance toward her bridegroom and her courage nearly fails . . . ) Zhukovsky, on the other hand, showed emotional experience in its inward, not outward manifestations, as a kind of state of soul."[18]

Both these principles—harmonization and the evocation of the inward through the outward—were Batyushkov's artistic discoveries. With their help he completely rebuilt the poetry of the literary school from which he himself had emerged: the school of Karamzin and Dmitriev.

Batyushkov appreciated the originality and followed in the footsteps of the playwright Vladislav Ozerov, of whose works he was extremely fond, and whom he knew personally from the circle of Alexey Olenin. In a poem dedicated to Semenova, the actress who played the leading parts in Ozerov's tragedies, Batyushkov wrote in 1809, apropos her performance as Xenia in the tragedy *Dmitry of the Don* (*Dmitry Donskoy*):

> All warring passions find in her a dread commingling
> I saw and felt the soul's abundance that she voiced
> And in this dream rejoiced.[19]

Ozerov united such renderings of the bewildering battle of contradictory emotions with the elaboration of elegiac themes: "The monologues of Fingal, Dmitry, Pollax are full of elegiac formulae: declarations of love, separations, untimely deaths . . . Their place is among the elegies of Batyushkov, Gnedich, and Zhukovsky."

The elegiac rendering of love which Batyushkov had seen in the tragedies of Ozerov was incorporated into his elegies, but was completely transformed in the process; Batyushkov's work on the elegiac genre was toward an inner dramatization; he introduced inward drama into the elegy expressed by the dynamic use of words.

In distinction from Ozerov, Batyushkov concentrated entirely on the artistic representation of the inner promptings of the heart and mind, on the evocation of the emotional life of the individual, on the study of what he called the "heart," as opposed to reason, that is, to the intellectual content of human consciousness.

As a result of a profound and thoughtful survey of the heritage of the eighteenth century, its philosophical thought and historical and ethical theories, Batyushkov, like others active in the Romantic movement—like Madame de Staël and Chateaubriand in France, like his own friend Zhukovsky—became convinced of the untenability of all the rationalistic theories of the eighteenth century in what for him was the cardinal question: their explanation of man.

Batyushkov came to the conclusion that man is not altogether knowable, that he cannot be reduced to any one definite system capable of classifying his abilities and properties. Man, for him, is a

whole world of complex, self-contradictory feelings and aspirations—
a world which may not be finally penetrated either by science or by
art.

Poetry, Batyushkov thought, can only guess what is going on in
man's inner self, and he preferred to elaborate a poetic word-portrait
of the outward as a reflection of the inner world of man, leaving the
deepest, inmost motives unnamed, to be guessed at and assumed.

Batyushkov saw in his system of harmonization, in direct
contrast to the strict defenders of the Classicist aesthetic, a rational
means of conveying the irrational and, in the last analysis, unknow-
able essence of man's "heart."

A study of Batyushkov's social prerequisites and literary sources
—intertwined with the general development of aesthetic thought,
his own poetry, the artistic practice of Russian poetry of his
time—would permit us to define the place occupied in the history
of Russian literature by the "school of harmonious precision" in
general and by Batyushkov in particular, to see how those works re-
late to the literary trends of the age.

Having destroyed and invalidated the mechanical conception of
man, Batyushkov elaborated two genres which were new to Russian
poetry: the epistle and the elegy. His elegies, having assimilated
the experience of Ozerov's tragedies, acquired the ability to portray
dramatic moments of man's inner life through their exterior expression by words and style (precision), intensified by a carefully or-
chestrated sound structure (harmonization), intended to add an
emotional perspective to what must, in man, remain outside the
cognitive scope of reason.

All this contributes to establish the organic unity of style and
content in Batyushkov's poetry and to fix his place side by side with
Zhukovsky at the source of the Russian Romantic movement as one
of the two creators of Romantic psychologism in Russian literature
during the second decade of the nineteenth century.

# Notes and References

## Preface

1. V. G. Belinskii, *Polnoe sobranie sochinenii* (Moscow: Izdatel'stvo Akademii Nauk SSSR, 1955), VII, 252. (Hereafter cited as: V. G. Belinskii)

## Chapter One

1. K. N. Batiushkov, *Sochineniia, so stat'eiu o zhizni i sochineniiakh,* napisannoi L. N. Maikovym, i primechaniiami, sostavlennymi im zhe i V. I. Saitovym (St. Petersburg, 1887), III, 87. (Hereafter cited as: Batiushkov, *Sochineniia*)

2. *Ibid.,* III, 8.

3. *Ibid.,* 158.

4. Evariste Parny, *Oeuvres choisies* (Paris, 1836), p. 82. (Hereafter cited as: Parny)

5. Batiushkov, *Polnoe sobranie stikhotvorenii,* Vstupitel'naia stat'ia podgotovka teksta i primechaniia N. V. Fridmana. Biblioteka poeta, Bol'shaiia seriia, vtoroe izdanie. (Moscow-Leningrad: Izdatel'stvo "Sovetskii pisatel'," 1964), p. 59. (Hereafter cited as: Batiushkov, *Stikhotvoreniia*)

6. A. M. Kukulevich, *Russkaia idilliia N. I. Gnedicha "Rybaki,"* Uchenye zapiski Leningradskogo gosudarstvennogo universiteta, Seriia filologicheskikh nauk, vypusk 3 (Leningrad, 1935), pp. 312–320. (Hereafter cited as: A. M. Kukulevich)

7. N. I. Gnedich, "Rassuzhdenie o prichinakh, zamedliaiushchikh uspekhi nashey slovesnosti," in *Opisanie torzhestvennogo otkrytiia Publichnoy biblioteki* (St. Petersburg, 1814), pp. 82–83.

8. *Ibid.,* p. 80.

9. Gnedich, *Sochineniia* (SPb.-M.), 1884, I, 194.

10. Kukulevich, p. 286.

11. Batiushkov, *Sochineniia,* III, 16.

12. *Ibid.,* p. 14.

13. *Ibid.,* p. 12.

14. *Ibid.,* p. 30.

15. *Ibid.,* p. 13.

16. *Ibid.,* p. 6.

17. *Ibid.*

18. *Ibid.,* p. 8.

19. *Ibid.*

20. Chandler B. Beall, *La fortune de Tasse en France* (Eugene, Oregon, 1942), p. 201.

21. *Ibid.,* p. 262–263.

22. Batiushkov, *Stikhotvoreniia,* p. 72.

23. Batiushkov, *Sochineniia,* II, 156.

24. *Ibid.,* p. 318.

25. Anne Louise Germaine De Staël-Holstein, *De la littérature...* (Paris, 1858), pp. 156–157. (Hereafter cited as: De Staël)

26. Batiushkov, *Sochineniia,* II, 151–152.

### Chapter Two

1. S. A. Shikhmatov, *Pesn' rossiiskomu slovu* (St. Petersburg, 1809). (Hereafter cited as: S. Shikhmatov)

2. Batiushkov, *Stikhotvoreniia,* p. 95. Here and elsewhere, with the exception of cases specifically noted, the *italics* are my own. I.S.

3. *Ibid.*

4. *Ibid.*

5. Shikhmatov, pp. 23–24.

6. *Ibid.,* p. 24.

7. Batiushkov, *Stikhotvoreniia,* p. 100.

8. Shikhmatov, *Pozharskii, Minin, Germogen ili spasennaia Rossiia* (St. Petersburg, 1807), p. 15.

9. Batiushkov, *Stikhotvoreniia,* p. 100.

10. *Ibid.*

11. Letter from Gnedich to Batiushkov, December 6, 1809. In Manuscript Department, Institute of Russian Literature (Pushkin House), AN SSSR, Razriad 1, Opis' 5.

12. Batiushkov, *Sochineniia,* III, 81.

13. Letter from Gnedich to Batyushkov, February 10, 1810. In Manuscript Department, Institute of Russian Literature (Pushkin House), AN SSSR, Razriad 1, Opis' 5.

14. Batiushkov, *Sochineniia,* III, 82–83.

15. *Ibid.,* pp. 75–86.

16. *Ibid.,* p. 86.

17. A. S. Shishkov, *Perevod dvukh statei iz Lagarpa* (St. Petersburg, 1808), p. XIII.

18. S. Glinka, "Fedor Mikhailovich Rtishchev," *Russkii vestnik,* 1809, No. 4, pp. 21–22.

19. *Ibid.*

20. Batiushkov, *Sochineniia*, III, 56–57.

21. Batiushkov, *Sochineniia*, Vstupitel'naia stat'ia, podgotovka teksta i primechaniia L. A. Ozerova. (Moscow: Gosudarstvennoe izdatel'stvo khudozhestvennoi literatury, 1955), p. 308. (Hereafter cited as: Batiushkov, *Sochineniia*, 1955)

22. Batiushkov, *Sochineniia*, 1955, pp. 308–309.

23. N. V. Fridman, *Proza Batiushkova* (Moscow: Izdatel'stvo "Nauka," 1965), pp. 60–61.

24. Batiushkov, *Sochineniia*, 1955, pp. 307–308.

25. *Ibid.*, p. 329.

26. *Ibid.*, p. 363.

27. *Ibid.*, p. 366.

28. *Ibid.*, pp. 367–368.

29. Batiushkov, *Sochineniia*, III, 56–57.

30. Batiushkov, *Sochineniia*, 1955, p. 319.

31. *Ibid.*, p. 322.

### Chapter Three

1. Batiushkov, *Sochineniia*, III, 39.

2. Batiushkov, *Sochineniia*, Redaktsiia, vstupitel'naia stat'ia i kommentarii D. D. Blagogo (M.—L.: Izdatel'stvo "Academia," 1934), pp. 529–530. (Hereafter cited as: Batiushkov, *Sochineniia*, 1934)

3. Batiushkov, *Stikhotvoreniia*, p. 95.

4. *Ibid.*, p. 98.

5. *Ibid.*, p. 96.

6. *Ibid.*, p. 101.

7. Batiushkov, *Sochineniia*, III, 47.

8. Batiushkov, *Sochineniia*, 1955, p. 382.

9. *Ibid.*, p. 383.

10. Batiushkov, *Stikhotvoreniia*, p. 79.

11. A. S. Shishkov. *Rassuzhdeniia o starom i novom sloge rossiiskogo iazyka* (St. Petersburg, 1803), pp. 157–158.

12. Batiushkov, *Sochineniia*, 1934, p. 450.

13. Parny, p. 404.

14. *Ibid.*, p. 403.

15. *Ibid.*

16. Charles-Hubert Millevoye, *Oeuvres* (Paris, 1816), Part 1, pp. 9–10.

17. *Ibid.*, p. 32.

18. *Ibid.*, p. 34.

19. I. T. Dmitriev, *Polnoe sobranie strikhotvorenii*, Biblioteka poeta, Bol'shaia seriia, 2-oe izd. (Leningrad: Izdatel'stvo "Sovetskii pisatel', " 1967), p. 144. (Hereafter cited as: Dmitriev)

20. Batiushkov, *Sochineniia,* 1934, p. 455.
21. *Ibid.*
22. Batiushkov, *Stikhotvoreniia,* p. 102.
23. Batiushkov, *Stikhotvoreniia,* p. 114.
24. Nice Contieri. "Batyushkov e il Petrarca." In *Annali,* Sezione Slava (Napoli, 1959), v. II, pp. 168–169.
25. *Ibid.,* pp. 169–171.
26. Batiushkov, *Sochineniia,* 1955, p. 373.
27. *Ibid.,* p. 375.
28. *Ibid.,* pp. 376–77.
29. *Ibid.* p. 384.
30. De Staël. pp. 278–279.
31. Letter from Gnedich to Batiushkov, March 21, 1811. In Manuscript Department, Institute of Russian Literature (Pushkin House), AN SSSR, Razriad I, Opis' 5.
32. Batiushkov, *Stikhotvoreniia,* p. 284.
33. Batiushkov, *Sochineniia,* III, 117.
34. Voltaire, *Oeuvres* (Paris, 1846), VIII, p. 5.
35. Batiushkov, *Sochineniia,* III, 141.
36. Dmitriev, p. 359.
37. *Ibid.,* p. 360.
38. Parny, p. 430.
39. Batiushkov, *Stikhotvoreniia,* p. 117.
40. *Ibid.*
41. *Ibid.*
42. *Ibid.*
43. Letter from Gnedich to Batiushkov, December 16, 1810. In Manuscript Department, Institute of Russian Literature (Pushkin House), AN SSSR, Razriad I, Opis' 5.
44. A. S. Pushkin, *Polnoe sobranie sochinenii* (Moscow: Izdatel'stvo AN SSSR, 1937), 49, II, 496. (Hereafter cited as: Pushkin)
45. Batiushkov, *Stikhotvoreniia,* p. 111.
46. M. N. Murav'ev, *Stikhotvoreniia,* Biblioteka poeta, Bol'shaia seriia (Leningrad: Izdatel'stvo "Sovetskii pisatel'," 1967), p. 235.
47. Batiushkov, *Stikhotvoreniia,* p. 111.
48. Parny, p. 7.
49. *Ibid.,* p. 8.
50. Batiushkov. *Stikhotvoreniia,* p. 111.
51. *Ibid.,* pp. 111–112.
52. *Ibid.,* p. 120.

174 KONSTANTIN BATYUSHKOV

Chapter Four

1. Batiushkov, *Sochineniia*, III, 81.
2. *Ibid*, p. 77.
3. B. Tomashevskii, *Pushkin, Kniga pervaya* (1813–24) (M.-L.: Izdatel'stvo AN SSSR, 1956), p. 74. (Hereafter cited as: Tomashevskii)
4. Batiushkov, *Stikhotvoreniia*, pp.287–288.
5. *Ibid.*, p. 138.
6. Batiushkov, *Sochineniia*, II, 739.
7. Batiushkov, *Stikhotvoreniia*, p. 140.
8. *Ibid.*
9. P. A. Viazemskii, *Polnoe sobranie sochinenii* (St. Petersburg, 1880), III, 99. (Hereafter cited as: Viazemskii)
10. V. A. Zhukovskii, *Polnoe sobranie sochinenii* (St. Petersburg, 1902), I, 104. (Hereafter cited as: Zhukovskii)
11. Pushkin, I, 72.
12. *Vestnik Evropy*, 1819, Part 103, No. 8.
13. Batiushkov, *Sochineniia*, 1934, p. 480.
14. N. M. Karamzin, *Polnoe sobranie stikhotvorenii*, Biblioteka poeta, Bol'shaia seriia (M.-L.: Izdatel'stvo "Sovetskii pisatel'," 1966), p. 192.
15. *Ibid.*, p. 194.
16. See: E. N. Kupreianova, "Dmitriev i poety karamzinskoi shkoly," *Istoriia russkoi literatury* (M.-L.: Izdatel'stvo AN SSSR, 1941), V, 136.
17. Batiushkov, *Stikhotvoreniia*, p. 245.
18. Batiushkov, *Sochineniia*, 1955, p. 147.
19. V. Vinogradov. *Stil' Pushkina* (Moscow: Gosudarstvennoe izdatel'stvo khudozhestvenoi literatury, 1941), pp. 196–198.
20. B. L. Komarovich, "Pometki Pushkina v 'Opytakh' Batiushkova," *Literaturnoe Nasledstvo* (Moscow, 1934), No. 16–18, pp. 885–904.
21. Pushkin, XII, 272–273.
22. Batiushkov, *Stikhotvoreniia*, p. 134.
23. G. Gukovskii, *Pushkin i russkie romantiki* (Moscow: Gosudarstvennoe izdatel'stvo khudozhestvennoi literatury, 1965), pp. 231–239. (Hereafter cited as: G. Gukovskii)
24. *Son Voinov* is a translation from Parny.
25. Batiushkov, *Stikhotvoreniia*, p. 134.
26. *Ibid.*
27. *Ibid.*, pp. 134–140.
28. *Ibid.*, p. 137.
29. *Ibid.*, pp. 137–138.
30. Batiushkov, *Sochineniia*, III, 128.
31. *Ibid.*, p. 312.

32. Batiushkov, *Stikhotvoreniia*, p. 134.
33. *Ibid.*
34. *Ibid.*, p. 137.
35. *Ibid*, p. 117.
36. *Ibid.*, p. 141.
37. *Ibid.*
38. *Ibid.*, pp. 140–141.
39. *Ibid.*, p. 141.
40. *Ibid.*
41. *Ibid.*
42. *Ibid.*
43. *Ibid.*, pp. 134–141.
44. *Ibid.*, pp. 138–139.
45. *Ibid.*, pp. 140–141.
46. *Ibid.*, p. 137.

*Chapter Five*

1. Batiushkov, *Sochineniia*, III, 206.
2. *Ibid.*, pp. 251–252.
3. *Ibid.*, p. 209.
4. *Ibid.*, pp. 205–206.
5. Batiushkov, *Sochineniia*, II, 130.
6. *Ibid.*, pp. 131–132.
7. *Ibid.*, p. 133.
8. *Ibid.*, pp. 129–130.
9. *Ibid.*, p. 129.
10. Batiushkov, *Sochineniia*, III, 208–209.
11. Fridman, "Poslanie K. N. Batiushkova 'K Dashkovu,'" *Filologicheskie nauki* (Moscow, 1963), No. 4. p. 201.
12. Batiushkov, *Stikhotvoreniia*, p. 153.
13. *Ibid.*, p. 154.
14. Batiushkov, *Sochineniia*, II, 362.
15. Batiushkov, *Stikhotvoreniia*, p. 193.
16. *Ibid.*, p. 171.
17. *Ibid.*, pp. 221–222.
18. Batiushkov, *Sochineniia*, II, 460–461.
19. See: I. Z. Serman, "Poeziia K. N. Batiushkova," Uchenye zapiski Leningradskogo gosudarstvennogo universiteta. Filologicheskaia seriia, vypusk 3, No. 49 (Leningrad, 1939), p. 263.
20. Batiushkov, *Stikhotvoreniia*, p. 212.
21. *Ibid.*, pp. 217–218.

22. *Ibid.,* p. 218.

23. *Ibid.,* pp. 219–220.

24. Batiushkov, *Sochineniia,* III, 421.

25. *Ibid.,* p. 345.

26. *Ibid.,* p. 103.

27. *Ibid.,* p. 106.

28. *Ibid.,* p. 110.

29. M. Alpatov, *Stat'i i issledovaniia* (Moscow: Izdatel'stvo "Iskusstvo," 1968), II, 69.

30. *Ibid.,* p. 72.

31. Batiushkov, *Sochineniia,* II, 106.

32. *Ibid.,* p. 181.

33. *Ibid.,* p. 107.

34. Letter of November 27, 1816. See: *Otchet publichnoi biblioteki za 1895g.* (St. Petersburg, 1898), Prilozhenie, p. 23.

35. Batiushkov, *Stikhotvoreniia,* p. 308.

36. Charles Hubert Millevoye, *Oeuvres,* (Paris, 1835), p. 86. (Hereafter cited as: Millevoye)

37. Batiushkov, *Stikhotvoreniia,* p. 207.

38. Millevoye, p. 86.

39. Batiushkov, *Stikhotvoreniia,* p. 208.

40. Millevoye, p. 87.

41. Batiushkov, *Stikhotvoreniia,* p. 208.

42. M. V. Lomonosov, *Polnoe sobranie sochinenii* (M.-L.: Izdatel'stvo AN SSSR, 1959), p. 89. (Hereafter cited as: Lomonosov)

43. Batiushkov, *Stikhotvoreniia,* p. 206.

44. Millevoye, p. 85.

45. Batiushkov, *Stikhotvoreniia,* p. 208.

46. *Ibid.,* p. 207.

47. Batiushkov, *Sochineniia,* II, 239.

48. *Ibid.,* p. 240.

49. V. A. Ozerov, *Tragedii i stikhotvoreniia,* Biblioteka Poeta, Bol'shaia seriia (Leningrad: Izdatel'stvo "Sovetskii pisatel'," 1960), p. 170.

50. Batiushkov, *Sochineniia,* II, 241.

51. Parny, p. 438.

52. Batiushkov, *Stikhotvoreniia,* p. 117.

53. Petrarca, *Le Rime,* (Parma, 1790), I, 130.

54. Batiushkov, *Stikhotvoreniia,* p. 114.

55. *Ibid.,* p. 164.

56. *Ibid.,* p. 167.

57. L. S. Fleyshman, "Iz istorii elegii v pushkinskuiu epokhu," *Pushkinskii sbornik* (Riga, 1968), p. 30. (Hereafter cited as Fleyshman)

58. *Ibid.*, p. 31.
59. Batiushkov, *Stikhotvoreniia*, p. 194.
60. Millevoye, pp. 15–16.
61. Batiushkov, *Stikhotvoreniia*, p. 190.
62. Lomonosov, VIII, 361.
63. Pushkin, XII, 260.
64. Batiushkov, *Stikhotvoreniia*, p. 79.
65. *Ibid.*, p. 196.
66. *Ibid.*
67. Gukovskii, p. 100.
68. Batiushkov, *Stikhotvoreniia*, p. 197.
69. Yurii Tynianov, *Arkhaisty i novatory* (Leningrad: Izdatel'stvo "Priboi," 1929), p. 257.

### Chapter Six

1. L. N. Maikov, *Batiushkov, ego zhizn' i sochineniia*, Izdanie vtoroe, (St. Petersburg, 1896), p. 141. (Hereafter cited as: Maikov)
2. *Ibid.*, p. 137.
3. Batiushkov, *Sochineniia*, II, 175.
4. *Ibid.*, p. 171.
5. Batiushkov, *Stikhotvoreniia*, pp. 191–192.
6. *Ibid.*, p. 279.
7. P. Tikhonov, *Nikolai Ivanovich Gnedich* (St. Petersburg, 1884), p. 3.
8. See: N. V. Fridman, "Tvorchestvo Batiushkova v otsenke russkoi kritiki 1817–20 gg.", Uchenye zapiski Moskovskogo universiteta, Trudy kafedry russkoi literatury, vypusk 127 (Moscow, 1948), pp. 179–200. (Hereafter cited as Fridman)
9. *Ibid.*, p. 180.
10. *Ibid.*, p. 181.
11. *Ibid.*, p. 186.
12. *Ibid.*
13. *Ibid.*, p. 187.
14. Batiushkov, *Sochineniia*, III, 459.
15. *Ibid*, pp. 447–448.
16. Batiushkov. *Stikhotvoreniia*, p. 192.
17. Batiushkov, *Sochineniia*, 1934, p. 440.
18. Batiushkov, *Stikhotvoreniia*, p. 192.
19. Parny, pp. 403–404.
20. Batiushkov, *Stikhotvoreniia*, p. 192.
21. *Ibid.*
22. *Ibid.*, p. 198.

23. *Ibid.*, p. 208.

24. *Vestnik Evropy*, 1819, Part 103, No. 8.

25. Batiushkov, *Sochineniia*, III, 459.

26. *Ibid.*, pp. 447–448.

27. *Ibid.*, pp. 417, 453–356.

28. *Arzamas i arzamsskie protokoly*, Vvodnaia stat'ia, redaktsiia protokolov i primechaniia k nim M. S. Borovkoi-Maikovoi, predislovie D. Blagogo (Leningrad: Izdatel'stvo Pisatelei v Leningrade, 1933).

29. Batiushkov, *Sochineniia*, III, 382.

30. *Ibid.*, pp. 438–439.

31. *Ibid.*, p. 439.

32. *Ibid.*

33. Karamzin, *Sochineniia* (St. Petersburg, 1849), III, 701.

34. Belinskii, V, 254.

35. Batiushkov, *Stikhotvoreniia*, p. 230.

36. *Ibid.*, pp. 229–230.

37. *Ibid.*, p. 233.

38. L. Ya. Ginzburg, *O lirike* (M.-L.: Izdatel'stvo "Sovetskii pisatel'," 1964), pp. 25–30.

39. Fridman, pp. 197–198.

40. Batiushkov, *Stikhotvoreniia*, p. 232.

41. Fridman, p. 198.

42. Batiushkov, *Stikhotvoreniia*, p. 238.

43. *Ibid.*, p. 236.

44. Belinskii, V, 254.

45. *Ibid.*, VII, 224.

46. A. Galakhov, *Istoriia russkoi slovesnosti, drevnei i novoi* (St. Petersburg, 1880), II p. 271.

47. Gukovskii, pp. 167–168.

48. Batiushkov, *Sochineniia*, III, 556.

49. *Ibid.*, p. 781.

50. Letter of January 13, 1821, in *Vospominaniia i rasskazy deiatelei tainykh obshchestv 1820-kh gg.* (Moscow, 1931), I, 146.

51. Viazemskii, 1883, VIII, 481.

52. E. N. Kupreianova, "E. A. Baratynskii," *E. A. Baratynskii: Polnoe sobranie stikhotvorenii*, Biblioteka poeta, (Leningrad: Izdatel'stvo "Sovetskii pisatel'," 1957), p. 16.

53. Fleyshman, pp. 24–54.

54. *Syn otechestva*, 1823, No. 1, p. 12.

55. O. Somov, "O romanticheskoi poezii," *Sorevnovatel' prosveshcheniia i blagotvoritel'nosti*, 1823, Part 24, Book 2, p. 145.

56. Wilhelm Küchelbecker, in *Mnemozina*, 1824, Part II, pp. 36–37.

57. *Ibid.*, p. 34.
58. Tomashevskii, pp. 114–115.
59. Pushkin, II, 58.
60. Ginzburg, pp. 210–212.
61. Pushkin, II, p. 50.
62. *Ibid.*
63. Batiushkov, *Sochineniia,* III, 491.
64. Maikov, p. 196.
65. *Ibid.*
66. See: D. D. Blagoi, *Tvorcheskii put' Pushkina (1813–1826)* (M.-L.: Izdatel'stvo AN SSSR, 1950), p. 235.
67. Fridman, p. 198.
68. Tomashevskii, pp. 324–325.
69. Batiushkov, *Stikhotvoreniia,* p. 199.
70. *Ibid,* p. 194.
71. Pushkin, XI, 157.
72. Batiushkov, *Stikhotvoreniia,* p. 221.
73. Tomashevskii, p. 527.
74. A. N. Maikov, *Polnoe sobranie sochinenii* (St. Petersburg, 1914) I, 9.
75. L. M. Lotman, "Liricheskaia i istoricheskaia poeziia 50–70kh godov," *Istoriia russkoi poezii v dvukh tomakh* (Leningrad: Izdatel'stvo "Nauka," 1969), I, 126.
76. A. A. Fet, *Polnoe sobranie stikhotvorenii,* Biblioteka poeta, (Leningrad: Izdatel'stvo "Sovetskii pisatel'," 1937), p. 144.
77. *Novyi mir,* 1932, No. 6.

## Conclusion

1. Batiushkov, *Sochineniia,* III, 447–448.
2. John Bowring (ed.), *Russian Anthology* (Boston, 1820). Republished as *Specimens of the Russian poets...,* translated by John Bowring, (Boston, 1882).
3. Aniela Kowalska, "John Bowring—tlumacz poetów Slowiańskich," *Slavis orientalis,* 1963, no. 1, pp. 51–83.
4. See: Chapter 6.
5. A. Bestuzhev, "Vzgliad na staruiu i novuiu slovesnost' v Rossii," *Poliarnaia zvezda na 1823 god* (St. Petersburg, 1823), p. 21.
6. Pushkin, XI, 110.
7. Ginzburg, p. 13–43.
8. *Ibid.,* p. 23.
9. Gukovskii, p. 173.
10. G. P. Makogonenko, "Poeziia Konstantina Batiushkova," *K. N.*

*Batiushkov, Stikhotvoreniia,* Biblioteka poeta, Malaia seriia, Izdanie tret'e (Leningrad: Izdatel'stvo "Sovetskii pisatel'," 1959), pp. 84–86.

11. Fridman, "Batiushkov i romanticheskoe dvizhenie," *Osnovnye problemy romantizma* (Moscow: Izdatel'stvo "Iskusstvo," 1968), pp. 92–93.

12. Batiushkov, *Sochineniia,* II, 340.

13. Pushkin, XII, 267.

14. Batiushkov, *Stikhotvoreniia,* p. 196.

15. Pushkin, XII, 267.

16. Vinogradov, pp. 181–182.

17. *Ibid.,* p. 184.

18. I. Semenko, "Pushkin i Zhukovskii," *Filologicheskie nauki* (Moscow, 1964), No. 4, p. 121.

19. Batiushkov, *Sochineniia,* 1955, p. 107.

# Selected Bibliography

### PRIMARY SOURCES

*Polnoe sobranie stikhotvorenii.* Vstupitel'naia stat'ia, podgotovka teksta i primechaniia N. V. Fridmana, Biblioteka poeta, Bol'shaia seriia, 2-oe izdanie. M.-L.: "Sovetskii Pisatel'," 1964.

*Sochineniia K. N. Batiushkova.* So stat'eiu o zhizni i sochineniiakh . . . napisannoiu L. N. Maikovym, i primechaniiami, sostavlennymi im zhe i V. I. Saitovym. 4 vols. St. Petersburg, 1885-87.

*Sochineniia.* Redaktsiia, stat'ia i kommentarii D. D. Blagogo. M.-L.: "Academia," 1934.

*Sochineniia.* Vstupitel'naia stat'ia L. A. Ozerova, podgotovka teksta i primechaniia N. V. Fridmana. Moscow: Gosizdat khudozhestvennoi literatury, 1955.

Batyushkov's Works Translated into English:

Coxwell, Ch. F. *Russian poems.* Introduction by D. Mirsky. London: Daniel, 1929.

*The Penguin Book of Russian Verse.* Introduced and edited by Dimitri Obolensky. Baltimore: Penguin Books, 1962.

*Specimens of the Russian poets.* Translated by John Bowring. Boston, 1822.

Wiener Leo. *Anthology of Russian Literature.* New York: Putnam, 1902-1903.

### SECONDARY SOURCES

BELINSKII, V. G. "Rimskie elegii Géte," *Polnoe sobranie sochinenii.* Moscow: AN SSSR, 1954. Vol. V, pp. 229-264.

———. "Sochineniia Aleksandra Pushkina." Stat'ia tret'ia, *Polnoe sobranie sochinenii.* Moscow: AN SSSR, Vol. VII, pp. 223-254.

FRIDMAN, N. V. "Batiushkov i romanticheskoe dvizhenie," Sbornik *Problemy romantizma.* Moscow: "Iskusstvo," 1967, pp. 70-102.

———. *Proza Batiushkova.* "Nauka," Moscow: 1965.

GINZBURG, L. *O lirike.* M.-L.: "Sovetskii pisatel'," 1964, pp. 22-43.

GUKOVSKII, G. *Pushkin i russkie romantiki.* Moscow Gosizdat khudozhestvennoi literatury, 1965, pp. 99-108, 164-172.

MAIKOV, L. *Batiushkov, ego zhizn' i sochineniia*, 2nd revised ed. St. Petersburg, 1896.

MAKOGONENKO, G. P. "Poeziia Konstantina Batiushkova," *K. N. Batiushkov, Stikhotvoreniia.* Biblioteka poeta, Malaia seriia, 3rd ed. Leningrad: "Sovetskii pisatel'," 1959, pp. 5-88.

SANDOMIRSKAIA, V. B. "K. N. Batyushkov," *Istoriia russkoi poezii v dvukh tomakh.* Vol. I. Leningrad: "Nauka," 1968, pp. 266-281.

SERMAN, I. Z. "Poeziia K. N. Batiushkova," Uchenye zapiski Leningrad-skogo gosudarstvennogo universiteta, No. 49. Filologicheskaia seriia No. 3, 1939, pp. 229-283.

TOMASHEVSKII, B. V. "K. N. Batiushkov," *K. N. Batiushkov, Stikhot-voreniia.* Biblioteka poeta, Malaia seriia, 2nd ed. Moscow: "Sovetskii pisatel'," 1948, p. V-LIX.

————. *Pushkin, Kniga Pervaia (1813-1824).* M.-L.: AN SSSR, 1956, pp. 56-71.

VERKHOVSKII, N. P. "Batyushkov," *Istoriia russkoi literatury.* M.-L.: AN SSSR, 1941, vol. V, pp. 392-417.

VINOGRADOV, V. V. *Stil' Pushkina.* Moscow: Gosizdat khudozhestvennoi literatury, 1941, pp. 171-198.

# Index

Akhmatova, Anna, 161–2
Alembert, Jean Le Rond d', 44
Alexander I (Tsar), 20–21, 35, 43, 128
Anacreon (-tics), 50, 51, 56
Antoninus, Marcus Aurelius, 107
Ariosto, 83
"Arzamas", 139–40

Baratynsky, Evgeny, 66, 138, 150–51, 152
Batyushkov, Alexandra Grigorevna (Konstantin's mother), 13
Batyushkov, Alexandra Nikolaevna (Konstantin's sister), 13, 23, 24
Batyushkov, Konstantin Nikolaevich (1787–1855): birth, 13; death of his mother, 13; predisposition to nervous ailments, 13; family of the old nobility, 13; childhood, 13; attends private school in Petersburg, 13–14; begins writing poetry, 14; works in Ministry of Public Education, 14–15; dislike of the civil service, 15; joins the "Free Society of Literature, Sciences and Arts," 15; verses begin to appear, 15; doubts of his talent and vocation, 18; interest in the theatre, 20–21; commissioned in the army, 21; wounded in battle, 21–22; service in Finland, 22; retires from army, 22; achieves poetical emancipation, 22; attainment of his own, individual style, 5–6, 23, 26, 47–71; translates Tasso, 26–30; a satirist, 31–45; extends literary acquaintance, works toward maturity, 72–92; works in the Public Library in Petersburg, 93; in Moscow during siege of 1812, 93–94; serves with General Raevsky, 94; feels strength and maturity of his talent, 94; gains recognition, 94, 102;

as elegist, 93–127; collects and revises his work, 128–42; his "anthological" verse, 142–49, 158–62; psychological problems, 132; works with the Russian mission in Naples, 149–50; psychological breakdown, 13, 150, 155; early conception of the poet-dreamer, 16–17; literary influences, 18–21; moral and religious views, 96–97; views on art, 106–108; views on social progress, 128–29; on language in poetry, 112–116, 120; his elegiac manner, 116–27, 169; care for unity of impression, 135; war in his poetry, 93–103; poetic use of history, 103–108; time in his elegies, 126–27; use of anaphora, 90–91, 102; "ideal form," 5, 6; "sculptural" quality of his verse, 148; evocation of the inward through the outward, 166–68; verse movement, 85–92; "harmonious precision," 164–69; influence on Pushkin, 152–58; influence at large, 162; significance, 5, 169

WORKS:

*Ariosto and Tasso,* 27, 29–30, 129
*Awakening (Probuzhdenie),* 137
*Bacchante,* 136, 159
*Bower of the Muses, The (Besedka muz),* 157–58
*Convalescence (Vyzdorovlenie),* 51–52, 120–23, 153
*Crossing of the Rhine, The (Perekhod cherez Reyn,* 101, 103–105
*Discourse in Praise of Sleep, A (Pokhval'noe slovo snu),* 129
*Discourse on the Influence of Light Verse on Language, A, (Rech'o*

183

# 186 KONSTANTIN BATYUSHKOV

Kapnist, 25, 49, 50, 67
Karamzin, Nikolay, 5, 6, 17, 18, 19, 25, 31, 32, 38, 43, 49, 51, 52, 72, 73, 74, 78–79, 85, 97, 141, 163, 168
Khemnitser, 33
Kheraskov, Mikhail Matveevich, 32, 33
Kiprensky, Orest Adamovich, 107–108
Knyazhnin, 20, 33
Komarovich, B. L., 81
Kozlov, V., 132
Krylov, Ivan Andreevich, 18, 25, 31, 36–37, 48, 67–68, 73, 93
Küchelbecker, Wilhelm, 146, 151–52, 155–56

La Fontaine, Jean de, 50, 134–35
La Harpe, Jean-François de, 31, 32, 38
Leibniz, Gottfried Wilhelm von, 128
Locke, John, 39
Lomonosov, Mikhail, 5, 31, 32, 33, 38, 43, 50, 61, 63, 73, 97, 111, 112, 120, 129, 130, 163
Lotman, L., 161

Makogonenko, G. P., 164
Mandelshtam, Osip, 162
Matveev, 39
Maykov, Apollon, 159, 160, 161
Maykov, L. N., 155
Merzlyakov, 31
Millevoye, Charles-Hubert, 56, 106, 109–12, 118–20, 138
Mirabeau, Comte de, 44
Montaigne, Michel Eyquem de, 96
Montesquieu, 42, 45, 128
Muraryov, Mikhail Nikitich, 14
Muraviev, Mikhail, 67, 78, 129
Muravieva, Ekaterina Fyodorovna, 93

Napoleon, 6, 20, 21, 22, 35, 39, 40, 46, 93, 95, 103, 128

Olenin, Alexey Nikolaevich, 18, 20, 25, 26, 36, 106, 107, 108, 111, 149, 168
Ossian, 16, 85
Ovid, 32, 55, 56, 59

Ozerov, Vladislav Alexandrovich, 18, 20, 21, 25, 112–13, 168, 169

Parny, Evariste, 16, 48, 49, 54, 55, 56, 59, 61–64, 65, 66–71, 83, 88, 113–14, 117, 134, 136, 152
Paul I (Tsar), 21
Peter I (Peter the Great), 39, 41, 42–43
Petrarch (-ism), 49, 54, 55, 58–59, 65, 74, 114, 134, 166
Piron, Alexis, 31–32
Pliny, 149
Plutarch, 109
Pnin, Ivan Petrovich, 15
poetry, 5, 16, 19, 28, 59, 60–61, 64–65, 77, 83, 85, 89, 125, 169; ode, 97–98, 111, 112, 117–18; narrative, 141, 153; epic, 19, 20, 26, 27, 28, 52, 65, 112, 140; elegy, 55, 56, 65, 97–127, 164, 168; "anthological," 142, 157, 158, 159, 160–62
poetry, French, 19, 55, 56, 65, 72
poetry, German, 19
poetry, Greek, 16, 18, 19–20
poetry, Italian, 29–30, 55, 165–66
poetry, Latin, 14, 16, 55, 56
poetry, Russian, 5, 6, 7, 17–20, 23, 26, 31, 32, 43, 49–52, 55, 59, 60–61, 65–66, 83, 97–98, 115–16, 117–18, 127, 133, 141, 142, 150–51, 152, 158, 159, 160, 161–62, 164, 165–66, 169
Propertius, 56
Pushkin, Alexander, 5, 66, 76–77, 80, 81–84, 97, 108, 116, 120, 127, 131, 140, 141, 149, 151, 152–58, 159, 160, 162, 164, 165–66, 167; *Prisoner of the Caucasus (Kavkazsky plennik)*, 127; *Ruslan and Lyudmila*, 153, 155
Pushkin, Vasily, 85

Racine, Jean, 38, 133
Radishchev, Alexander Nikolaevich, 15, 16
Radishchev, Nikolay Alexandrovich, 15
Raevsky, General Nikolay Nikolaevich, 94
Raphael Santi, 108

## ABOUT THE AUTHOR

Ilya Z. Serman is a Soviet scholar in the history of language and literature, a senior fellow of the Institute of Russian Literature attached to the Academy of Sciences of the USSR (Pushkin House). He is the author of the monographs "The Poetic Style of Lomonosov" (*Poeticheskiy stil' Lomonosova*) and "G.P. Derzhavin" and of various papers on the history of Russian Literature of the eighteenth and nineteenth centuries, such as "Trediakovsky and the Enlightenment" (*Trediakovsky i prosvetitel'stvo*), "Kantemir," "Sumarokov and his School" (*Sumarokov i ego shkola*), "Grand genre in the poetry of the 1770's" (*Bol'shaya forma v poezii 1770-kg. gg*), "Derzhavin," "The Poetry of V.V. Kapnist" (*Poeziya V.V. Kapnista*), "The Poetry of K.N. Batyushkov" (*Poeziya K.N. Batyushkova*), "Pushkin and historical drama in the 1830's" (*Pushkin i istoricheskaya drama 1830-kh gg.*) which appeared in the Academy of Sciences publications "The History of the Russian Novel" (*Istoriya russkogo romana*), "The History of Russian Poetry" (*Istoriya russkoy poezii*), "The Idea of Socialism in Russian Literature" (*Ideya sotsializma v russkoy literature*) and the periodical symposium "The XVIII Century" (*XVIII Vek*) of which he is one of the editors. He prepared the Volume of Bogdanovich's verse (*I. F. Bogdanovich. Stikhotvoreniya i poemy*) for the Large Series of "The Poet's Library" (*Biblioteka poeta*). Serman also contributed to the textological preparation and annotation of the collected works of Dostoyevsky and Leskov.